CW00793655

Fifth edition published in 2015 by MapStudio™ South Africa

ISBN (Print) 978-1-77026-783-1
ISBN (ePDF) 978-1-77026-797-8

Production Manager John Loubser
Project Manager Genené Hart
Designers Genené Hart, Nicole Bannister
Cartographers Genené Hart, Nicole Bannister
Reproduction Resolution Colours (Pty) Ltd, Cape Town
Marketing marketing@mapstudio.co.za
Feedback research@mapstudio.co.za
Photo credits © 2015 individual photographers as credited below:
Shaen Adey p2-3, 4-5, 12-13, 14 (bottom), 15, 17, 18, 19, 20, 22 (bottom), 23 (top), 24,
36 (bottom), 37, 39 (bottom), 41, 43, 50 (bottom), 51, 52, 53, 57, 58, 60, 62 (top), 67;
Dominic Barnardt p11 (top and bottom); Colour Library p40 (top), 71 (left);
Nigel J. Dennis p69; Gerhard Dreyer p 64, 65, 66; Jéan du Plessis p9 (top)
Iziko/William Fehr Collection p8 (top); Walter Knirr p22 (top), 36 (top), 46-47, 56 (bottom),
70 (bottom); Jacques Marais p10 (right); Peter Pickford p9 (bottom), 11 (middle), 49 (top);
Kristo Pienaar p45; South African National Library p8 (bottom); Erhardt Thiel p 14 (top),
23 (bottom), 25, 38, 50 (top), 62 (bottom); Hein von Horsten p21, 39 (top), 44, 48,
56 (top), 61 (bottom), 68 (bottom), 71 (right); Lanz von Horsten p40 (bottom), 59, 63;
Keith Young p61 (top); Chanan Weiss p10 (top and bottom left), 55
Printed and bound by Times Offset (M) Sdn. Bhd., Malaysia

MapStudio™
Unit 3, Block B, M5 Park
Eastman Road, Maitland, 7405
Tel: 0860 10 50 50, www.mapstudio.co.za

THE NAME YOU CAN TRUST
SINCE 1958

WESTERN CAPE

Contents

Introduction

Occupying the southern tip of the mega-continent, Africa, South Africa can match the best of them when it comes to contrasts in a single, unified land. 'Rainbow' nation? That it is, but not only in terms of its people; it is multi-hued also in terms of summer and winter, west coast and east coast, upland and lowland, mountain crest and shoreline. Of the nine provinces that glue together the jigsaw of this country's boundaries, Western Cape Province is arguably the one that attracts the most travellers and holidaymakers. The verdict depends on you, the visitors, to this green, fertile, river-dissected, rain-washed (and wind-blown) fruit- and bread-basket of South Africa. Climates in the Western Cape vary from the pretty-much rain-free and stony Namaqualand, to the truly Mediterranean hot-summer, rain-drenched-winter climate of Cape Town and its surrounds, up to the Garden Route's balmy, high-rainfall, temperate forest environs.

Covering two coastlines, the Western Cape enjoys massive geographical diversity, affording the area plenty of habitats, vegetation and landscapes.

Introduction

FIVE THINGS ANYONE CAN DO
- Ride an ostrich (Oudtshoorn)
- Enjoy the view from the top of Table Mountain (Cape Town)
- Smell the West Coast flowers
- Walk barefoot on one of the dozens of beaches along the coast
- Listen to the sounds of silence in one of the many natural areas

O lifants

Vanrhynsdorp

Vredendal

OLIFANTS RIVER VALLEY

Lambert's Bay

Clanwilliam

CEDERBERG

Dwarskersbos

St Helena Bay

Velddrif

WEST COAST & OLIFANTS

Vredenburg

Langebaan

Langebaan Lagoon

Berg

N7

Tulbagh

N1

THE BIG SIX
(See page 15)

Malmesbury

Ceres

BREEDE RIVER

Worcester

Kleinplasie

Durbanville

Wellington

Robertson

Montagu

Milnerton

Paarl

Robben Island

Stellenbosch

Franschhoek

McGregor

CAPE TOWN

Swell

Camps Bay

CAPE TOWN & WINELANDS

Hottentots
— Holland Nature
Reserve

Constantia

Hout Bay

Strand

Somerset West

Greyton

N2

Muizenberg

Boulders Beach

Gordon's
Bay

OVERBERG & BREEDE RIVER VALLEY

Simon's Town

Caledon

1-Robben Island
2-V&A Waterfront
3-Table Mountain
4-Kirstenbosch
5-Winelands
6-Cape Point

Table Bay

TO WINELANDS

False Bay

Hermanus

Stanford

Bredasdorp

Walker Bay

The Big 6 - Most visited

Cape Agulhas

A floral paradise, some of the Western Cape's most revered species include ericas, proteas and the more elusive – and spectacular – disa.

Introduction

FIVE ANIMALS TO SEE
- Whales along the coast
- Boulders Beach penguins
- Loeries in Knysna
- Cape Mountain Zebra in De Hoop Nature Reserve
- Birds on the West Coast

FIVE FAMOUS BUILDINGS TO VISIT
- Rhodes Memorial (Cape Town)
- The Taal Monument (Paarl)
- The Huguenot Monument (Franschhoek)
- The Castle of Good Hope (Cape Town)
- Buildings on Malmesbury's historic walk

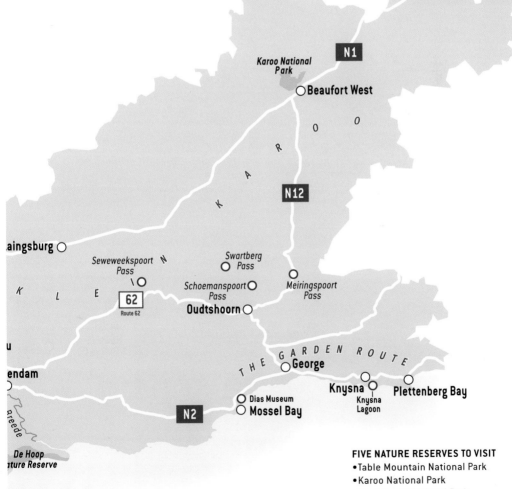

FIVE NATURE RESERVES TO VISIT
- Table Mountain National Park
- Karoo National Park
- West Coast National Park
- De Hoop Nature Reserve
- Cederberg Wilderness Area

History

Portrait of Jan van Riebeeck? Is this the real face of the founder of South Africa? The debate rages!

THE CAPE CULTURAL MIX

The earliest inhabitants of the southern tip of Africa were the San Bushmen, descendents of the Khoina peoples. Around 1000AD these Khoi-San were joined by migrating Bantu speakers who came from the north of the country. It was these cultural groups that Hollander Jan van Riebeeck encountered when his ship hit the shores of Table Bay. Today's Cape 'coloured' people are descended from the Khoina and the original Dutch settlers. After the arrival of the Dutch, newcomers to the fledgling colony arrived in the form of French and British settlers, as well as slaves and political refugees from Madagascar, Indonesia and Malaysia; indentured labourers from India later joined them. The British went on to make their mark after they took possession of the Cape permanently in 1806, leading to a major influx of British settlers in 1820.

A NEW COLONY ON THE WAY TO THE EAST

Cape Town began its lively existence in April 1652 as a halfway trading station. Lively? You have only to read the diaries of the genteel ladies who accompanied the early governors to gauge how the seeds of Cape Town's latent social merry-go-round were sown. 17-century traders of the Dutch East India Company, on their way to their colonies in the East, needed to replenish their fresh fruit and vegetable stores to stave off scurvy. The little settlement, headed up by its first Dutch commander, Jan van Riebeeck and his wife Maria de la Quellerie, soon swelled with the arrival (from 1688) of French Huguenots fleeing religious persecution in Europe. They penetrated inland of Table Bay, establishing themselves at the foot of a series of towering mountain ranges, where they tilled and terraced the fertile soils. Their enterprise was the halfway station's gain: their precious knowledge of the delectable juice of the vine laid the roots for the Cape's winelands.

THEN CAME THE BRITISH

The Dutch wielded their might for two centuries, but with the Netherlands' power declining towards the end of the 18th century, the British took the gap. The Cape became a Crown Colony in 1814 and self-government followed in 1872. Change came in 1910, when the four separate territories of the fledgling South Africa were unified, with the Cape colony becoming one of four official provinces. Cape Town was designated as the new nation's legislative capital, and retains this status to this day. South Africa was expelled from the Commonwealth (due to Apartheid) and became a republic in 1961.

Jan van Riebeeck met the local strandloper leader, Autshumao, when he landed in Table Bay to set up his Dutch refreshment station. Beads and trinkets were offered by the Dutch as a greeting.

History

APARTHEID – A DIRTY WORD

This truly South African term (literally meaning 'apart-ness') was created after 1948 when racial discrimi-nation laws were instituted by Dutch-born Hendrik Verwoerd, first as Minister of Native Affairs, and later as Prime Minister between 1958 and 1966 – the year he was assassinated. These laws prohibited mixed-race marriages, resulted in the loss of land and the estab-lishment of separate living areas for non-white cultural groups, removed the right to a proper education and restricted movement through the need to carry identity passes based on racial classification.

SEEING THE LIGHT

South Africa imprinted itself on the world's psyche in February 1990 when State President FW de Klerk unbanned the black parties (ANC, PAC and the Commu-nist Party) and released Nelson Mandela, up until then a high-profile political activist and founder of the ANC's military wing uMkhonte we Siswe. Mandela had been a prisoner of the state for 27 years since 1964, most of it spent on Robben Island. On 27 April 1994, with much rejoicing, South Africa voted the ANC into power (63% of the votes), and Nelson Mandela became the first black president of the 'New South Africa'. In 1999 Mandela stepped down, and was succeeded by Thabo Mbeki. Evan after his death in 2013, Mandela remains the country's great hero.

A RAINBOW NATION AND ITS CONSTITUTION

Former Anglican Archbishop Desmond Tutu, whose archdiocese was the City of Cape Town from 1986 (he has since relinquished his archbishopric), described the people of the 'new' South Africa (a term liberally peppering modern-day lingo, whether social or politi-cal) as 'the rainbow people of God'. It stuck, and the term Rainbow Nation has been sewn into the fabric of this land. Cape Town was the setting for the formula-tion of South Africa's Constitution, recognised as one of the world's most progressive; its Bill of Rights, which outlaws any discrimination in terms of ethnic or social origin, language, religion, gender or sexual orientation, is one of the most enlightened in existence today.

THE CAPE: CRADLE OF MANKIND?

At the turn of our new century, archaeologists made a historic find on the shores of Langebaan Lagoon, along the Cape's West Coast region. Tracks, in the form of fossilised footprints, were discovered in an outcrop of rock, dating back 117,000 years and representing the oldest form of the anatomically modern human being, Homo sapiens. These are believed to reinforce the theory that Africa is the cradle of mankind.

Nelson Mandela, one of the world's best-known faces and a universal icon for freedom and the fight for democratic change.

THE PEOPLE AND THE LINGO

With the transition from a white autocratic govern-ment to a multi-party democracy in 1994, the country legislated 11 official languages – English, Afrikaans, and nine Bantu tongues (including Zulu, Xhosa, Sotho and Tswana). Cape Town has a population of roughly four million, made up of 57% Cape 'coloured', 24% white, 18% black (mainly Xhosa-speaking) and 1% Asian.

A San bushman, descendant of the Khoina. Small groups of these hunter-gatherers still eke out an existence in parts of Namaqua-land and the Northern Cape today.

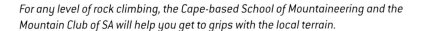

Activities

Rock climbing (above) requires precision and pluck, while kloofing (below) is one giant leap of faith.

WALKS AND ROCK CLIMBS

It all starts on that great monolith that forces itself on everyone's psyche when they're in Cape Town: Table Mountain. There are innumerable routes on every face of this mountain that can be tackled on two feet; or with the aid of knees, toes and fingernails; or hanging suspended from a strong (you hope!) rope. Books, route pamphlets or Cape Town Tourism will direct you to the myriad options. Further afield of the mountain, Lion's Head and the Twelve Apostles, there is no lack of towering rockscapes to explore, starting in the Winelands region.

HIKING AND KLOOFING

With so many mountains and valleys in Cape Town's backyard, there is a plethora of one-to eight-day hiking trails. Paths and routes are marked out through state reserves, private wilderness areas and small farms, many with basic overnight huts with minimal cooking and ablution facilities. Maps are provided with individual permits. Some of the best include the Otter, Tsitsikamma and Outeniqua trails, but if you like to get your feet wet, go kloofing in river valleys like Jonkershoek and Riviersonderend. Following the river, you can wade, boulder-hop and yell in primeval fashion while making a quantum leap into some of the mountain pools.

BIRD'S EYE VIEWS OF CITY- AND LANDSCAPES

When we say the world is your oyster, we mean it. Try a helicopter flip for size. Leaving from a helipad at the Waterfront, you'll see airborne perspectives of That Mountain, Cape Point or the Winelands that are guaranteed to change your worldview. Or you could drift over inland vine-terraces under the rainbow bubble of a hot-air balloon. If it's adrenaline you're seeking, the world of aero sports awaits you on the Cape's mountain heights, from Table Mountain to the Twelve Apostles, Lion's Head, Sir Lowry's Pass, Du Toit's Kloof Pass, and way beyond. Hang-gliders and para-gliders are constantly leaping off terra firma with wild abandon and, further inland, a small airfield base offers training courses for wannabe parachutists.

Mountain biking near Stellenbosch.

SPINNING ABOUT ON TWO WHEELS

Once again spoilt for choice with the Cape's mountain terrain, cyclists and mountain bikers have no cause to complain. In the more rugged wineland zones, a spider web of routes in the Breede River valley connect Worcester, Robertson and Montagu; the hot, dry Citrusdal landscape is freshened by the Olifants River and Cederberg mountains; De Hoop on the southern Cape coast has high dunes and wave-washed shores; and if you've had enough of blue skies, the Garden Route's hardwood forests around Kranshoek and Diepwalle Forest Station will give you plenty of branches to duck under and knobbly roots to fly over.

Activities

Big wave surfing at Dungeons, near Hout Bay.

BOUNCING ABOUT ON FOUR WHEELS

Word has it that some of the 4x4 trails laid out in the not-to-be-sneered-at Cape mountainscapes have rattled the most hardened of would-be Camel Man adventurers. The list of possibilities is endless: Montagu has the Langeberg range; Robertson, Greyton and McGregor the Riviersonderend mountains; Worcester and Ceres, the Hex River; Wellington, the Dutoitskloof mountains; while Stellenbosch and Somerset West boast the Helderberg and Hottentots Holland ranges. Penetrating into Karoo territory is the awe-inspiring Swartberg. Take your pick ... and hold your breath.

MESSING ABOUT IN H2O

Cape Town is not short of windy days, particularly when the southeaster blows into town. Windsurfers can jump waves at Muizenberg or Fish Hoek in False Bay, or skate across calmer surfaces on lagoons or inland bodies of water such as Seekoevlei, Rietvlei, Milnerton Lagoon or Langebaan. Kayakers, too, have the best of both worlds – miles and miles of west and east coast shoreline, or any one of the numerous protected lagoons. There are also multi-day organised expeditions, and plenty of local outfits who earn their keep by hiring out equipment and sharing their expertise.

FUN ON A WHITE-WATER RAFT

You can plunge into different degrees of white water (on a raft, of course) depending on the river and time of year. Multi-day expeditions on two- and eight-person inflatable rafts navigate sections of the Orange River (in the extreme north) and the Breede for wild-water running or quiet paddling, depending on your courage levels. This comes with experienced guides, equipment and great meals, while the evenings are spent under a canopy of stars. If you merely want to test the waters, the Breede offers a lazy Winelands canoe day-trip in the Worcester area, with historic homesteads, wine-tasting and riverbank picnics.

FROM ADRENALINE...

If your ticker needs a little speed therapy, you won't be able to resist a steel cage dive in the cold, deep, offshore Cape waters to meet a Great White Shark eyeball-to-massive-eyeball. Attracted by bait trailed behind the boat, you'll be wetsuited and safely ensconced inside the cage while they thrash at the grub around you, hopefully remaining outside the cold steel bars.

... TO COMATOSE

After this, your idea of fun will almost certainly be to sink your butt onto something comfortable and let the world slip by. You could put that same butt into a saddle and go ambling along the eternally beautiful sugar-sands of Noordhoek Beach and be whispered to by the waves; or wander on horseback through leafy vines in the shadow of a jagged mountain skyline on a graceful wine farm. Alternatively, catch a steam train the old-fashioned way and huff and puff to Spier Estate for the day.

Windsurfing (above) and kite surfing (bottom) are popular at Bloubergstrand beach, which is whipped by strong coastal winds.

Cape Town

The Cape Winelands

Cape Town

Africa being Africa (whopping distances across great undeveloped tracts and a not-so-developed transport infrastructure), you need your own vehicle if you'd like to do justice to your explorations. Beg, borrow or hire one – there's no need to steal, as there are plenty of car-hire companies operating at airports and in the major towns. It can't be ignored: mileage between major towns (and therefore between tourist sites), distances between scenic vistas, treks between windy and sheltered beaches, and even the hop from one watering hole to the next, simply can't be achieved on the existing bus and rail system. Yes, there is a pretty decent rail-line linking all of the Southern Suburbs' towns between Cape Town and Simon's Town; yes, round-trip buses ferry visitors between the city centre and the Waterfront area; and the 3-wheeled Rikki taxis can be called up at a moment's notice for short city-based trips. But this ain't gonna get you to Hout Bay and Chapman's Peak, Cape Point, the Winelands or up the West Coast to Namaqualand. Of course, there are many organised coach tours that will take you all the way up to the Garden Route and beyond – if that's the kind of trip that turns you on. So ... the choice is yours.

Top left: Minstrels in full dress.
Left: Touring bus on Signal Hill.

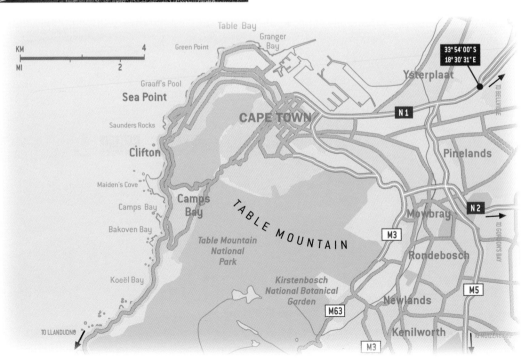

Cape Town is a cosmopolitan city with a wide range of architectural influences. Concrete fundis will enjoy her contemporary and unusual constructions.

Cape Town

THE BIG SIX

Cape Town is famous for many world-class attractions, but the Big Six of most-visited destinations is made up of the following:

1. Robben Island
   Walk in Nelson Mandela's footsteps.
2. V&A Waterfront
   Hop, shop and bop to your heart's content.
3. Table Mountain
   Get an eyeful of Cape Town from the summit.
4. Kirstenbosch National Botanical Garden
   Kick back and relax amidst the floral fragrances and rolling lawns.
5. Winelands
   A powerful magnet for most tourists: great grapes and a fun day of estate-hopping.
6. Cape Point
   Pristine beaches, fabulous fynbos and a dramatic and treacherous coastline washed by mighty waves.

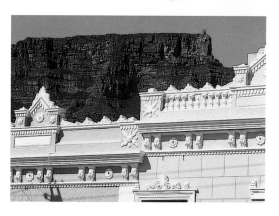

The Bo-Kaap is the seat of local Malay culture. Some homes date back to around 1810, and many feature ornate parapets and plasterwork.

> **Top Tip**
> Much of Cape Town and surrounds can be accessed via three main highways: the N1 leads to Paarl (and, ultimately, Joburg), the N2 (Airport Road) leads to the Garden Route, while the N7 takes you to the West Coast. The M3 links the City Bowl and the Cape Peninsula.

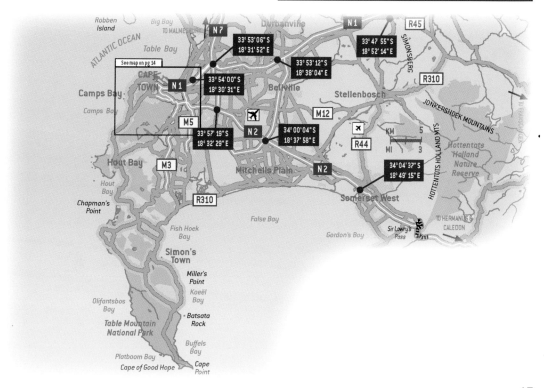

Get cosmic and climb Lion's Head at Full Moon in summer: watch the yellow moon rise as the red sun sets. Unforgettable – just don't forget to take a torch!

Cape Town

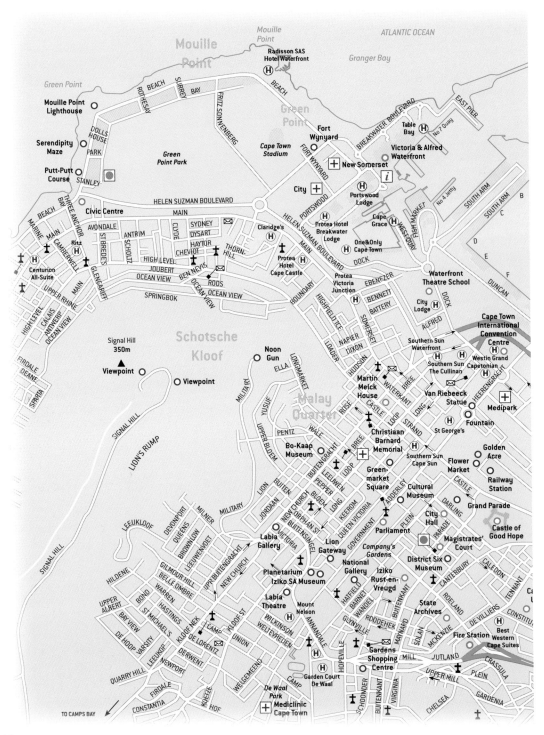

Cape Town

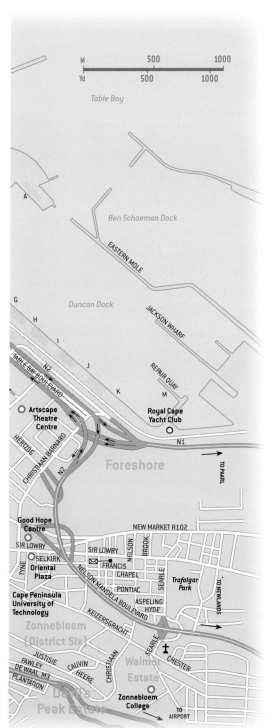

Table Mountain watches over the Waterfront.

Sandwiched between Table Bay and Table Mountain, the Atlantic prevents the city from expanding: mind you, land has already been reclaimed from the harbour to accommodate a growing metropolis that began life as Jan van Riebeeck's refreshment station. The city foreshore and ever-evolving V&A Waterfront complex are built on foundations that have been snatched back from the ocean.

NO TIME TO WASTE

If the Southeaster's not doing a Marilyn Monroe 'thang' on you, let the cableway (360° views from a revolving floor) whisk you to the top of the mountain in a couple of minutes; or walk up Long Street to marvel at the filigreed Victorian balconies and oodles of nightlife (lord it up in Kennedy's Cigar Lounge). Trawl Greenmarket Square's umbrella'd cobblestones for anything from African masks to beaded trinkets. Make for the Whale Well at the Iziko SA Musuem in the Company Gardens, where giant skeletons hang from the ceiling; be awed by the hi-tech projections of the Southern Hemisphere's night sky at the Planetarium. Then it's time to be posh: high tea at the gently pink Grande Dame, the Mount Nelson.

The cable car completes another round trip.

Cape Peninsula

Scenic view of the Cape Peninsula.

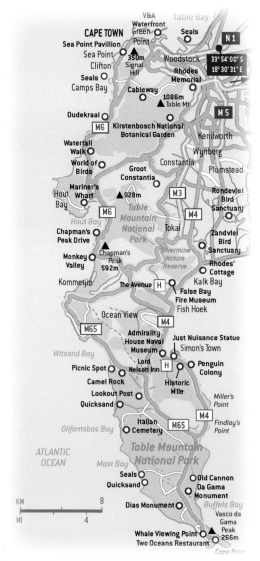

A 'TWEET' FOR ALL AGES

A visit to the World of Birds (on your way to Hout Bay and Chapman's Peak) is always a pleasure. This rehabilitation centre now has around 450 different species. Observe at your leisure (and sometimes from frighteningly close distances) Scarlet Ibis, Blue Crane, a flock of flamingoes and Egyptian Vultures. If you're brave you can eyeball some quizzical owls in the walkthrough cages: it's just you and the owls, so walk s-l-o-o-o-w! There are also porcupines, tortoises, marmosets, meerkats and monkeys to entertain and amuse the whole family.

GET TO THE POINT ... CAPE POINT

In the Cape of Good Hope (which forms part of the Table Mountain National Park) you're advised to roll up your windows against the chacma baboons, but keep your eyes peeled for eland, bontebok and other buck. At the parking area, the lazy ones can take the funicular, while the energetically inclined can walk to the view site to see Cape Point being battered by wild and restless seas. The Two Oceans restaurant here has stupendous views across False Bay, and there's an excellent visitors centre near the Dias Monument.

TABLE MOUNTAIN AND KIRSTENBOSCH

If you're of the fit-'n-active persuasion, thumb your nose at the cable car and tackle one of the myriad Table Mountain paths (easy and difficult) to the top, where the reservoirs are pretty and the views glorious. Kirstenbosch Botanical Garden offers you the birds and the bees — oh, and a massive array of trees and plants, not least of which is the lofty baobab in the glass conservatory. Rest ... and then 'do lunch' in the floor-to-ceiling-windowed restaurant. The Gardens also act as an outdoor art gallery, with scores of modern African sculptures decorating the lawns and flowerbeds.

Dias Monument, Cape Point.

Cape Peninsula

Table Mountain

1 Restaurant
2 Information Centre
3 Telephone
4 Public Toilets
5 Bridge
◯ Information Plaques

Cable Station

1067m

Viewpoint
(Platform)

Viewpoint
(Platform)

Viewpoint

Toilets

W E S T E R N   T A B L E

Fountain Ledge

Platteklip Buttress

Platteklip Gorge

Pumphouse (1928)
Viewpoint (Platform)

[Not to scale]

TO PLATTEKLIP
GORGE TRAIL &
WAR MEMORIAL

Right: Viewpoint on top of Table Mountain.

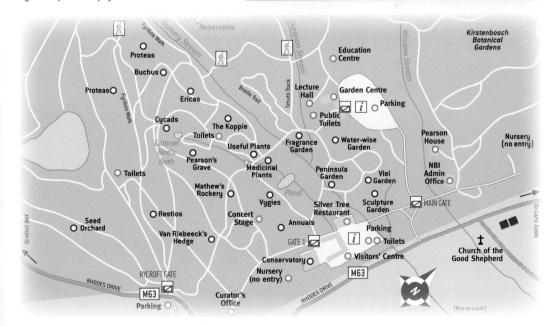

Reservoirs

Fynbos Walk

Nursery Stream

Skeleton Stream

Window Stream

Kirstenbosch
Botanical
Gardens

Proteas

Buchus

Proteas

Ericas

Braille Trail

Smuts Track

Education
Centre

Lecture
Hall

Garden Centre

Parking

Cycads

The Koppie

Toilets

Useful Plants

Public
Toilets

Fragrance
Garden

Water-wise
Garden

Pearson
House

Nursery
(no entry)

Colonel
Bird's
Bath

Pearson's
Grave

Medicinal
Plants

Peninsula
Garden

Vlei
Garden

NBI
Admin
Office

Toilets

Mathew's
Rockery

Pond

Vygies

Silver Tree
Restaurant

Sculpture
Garden

MAIN GATE

TO CAPE TOWN

Restios

Concert
Stage

Annuals

Parking

Seed
Orchard

Van Riebeeck's
Hedge

GATE 1

Toilets

Church of the
Good Shepherd

TO HOUT BAY

Conservatory

Visitors' Centre

RYCROFT GATE

Nursery
(no entry)

M63

RHODES DRIVE

M63

Parking

Curator's
Office

RHODES DRIVE

[Not to scale]

V&A Waterfront

It was Queen Victoria's son Prince Alfred who set into motion the building of Alfred Basin when he tumbled a load of rocks into the excavated sea floor of stormy Table Bay. Today, the Victoria and Alfred basins have morphed into the inexorably growing V&A Waterfront complex, a place for singing, laughing, drinking and eating – like that 'accessible' Graça wine. You can also do lots of shopping in chi-chi designer stores.

For a little excitement, test your nerves before the shatter-proof glass, 2-million-litre Predator Tank at the Two Oceans Aquarium. A glass-width away from the serrated jaws of ragged-tooth sharks, you can see yourself reflected back in their cold emotionless gaze. At specific times, it's feeding time at the zoo when divers in chain mail brave the tank to satiate the ferocious fishies' appetites. Don't miss it.

Finish the day with sundowners on the terrace of the Radisson Hotel in next-door Granger Bay – crashing waves, swooping gulls, pastel skies and catamarans gliding out to sea on a zephyr's breath. It's tough in Africa.

Nelson Mandela Gateway in the V&A Waterfront where the Ferry departs to Robben Island.

1 • Two Oceans Aquarium
2 • Watershed
3 • Iziko Maritime Centre
4 • V&A Food Market
5 • Robinson Dry Dock
6 • Alfred Basin
7 • V&A Hotel and Alfred Mall
8 • Pierhead
9 • New 7 Wonders Photo Frame
10 • Clocktower Square and Conference Centre
11 • Gateway to Robben Island
12 • Victoria Basin
13 • Penny Ferry
14 • National Sea Rescue Institute
15 • Quay Four
16 • Buses to the City
17 • Rugby Museum
18 • Union Castle Building
19 • Market Square
20 • Ferryman's Brewery
21 • Amphitheatre
22 • Victoria Wharf Shopping Centre
23 • Robben Island Museum
24 • Red Shed Craft Workshop
26 • New Somerset Hospital
27 • Portswood Lodge
28 • Portswood Square
29 • UCT Graduate School of Business
30 • Protea Hotel Breakwater Lodge
31 • Cape Grace Hotel
32 • Table Bay Hotel
33 • Bascule Bridge
34 • Waterfront Visitors Centre
35 • Seal Landing

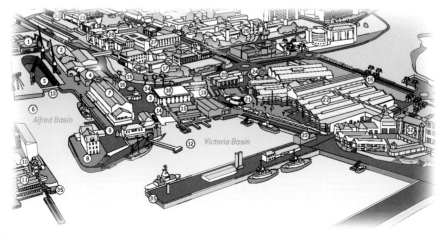

Nelson Mandela and seven other political activists were condemned to life imprisonment [on Robben Island], in the famous 1963 Rivonia Treason Trial.

Robben Island

A historical and ecological heritage site today [its seabird breeding colony is protected and in 1999 it was declared a World Heritage Site], Robben Island was named after its seal population [seals are 'robbe' in Dutch]. But it started its life as something much more sinister – it was a penal settlement as early as 1658, when Jan van Riebeeck banished his interpreter here. Under a more modern government it became a maximum-security prison in 1964, but its last political prisoners were all released in 1991.

The prison on Robben Island.

Robben Island is most famous for the barred hole-in-the-wall of Nelson Mandela's cell, behind which, in 1963, he was condemned to remain for 18 of his 23-year sentence. And it is in the island's blinding white lime quarries that Mandela's eyesight suffered early damage – prison inmates were forced to work there for six hours a day.

> ***Top Tip***
> *The 3-hour Robben Island round-trip is very popular and bookings are made at the Robben Island Museum, V&A Waterfront [book well in advance – preferably days!].*

Today, visitors are treated to a genuine first-hand account of life behind those forbidding walls through the eyes of ex-political inmates, who conduct a guided tour of the prison cells. A bus trip takes visitors to the quarry and other sites of interest around the island. Among these is the 18m-high [59ft] lighthouse, built in 1863 to replace the fire beacons once used to warn off sailors being tossed about on the high seas; its beam can be spotted 25km [16 miles] away.

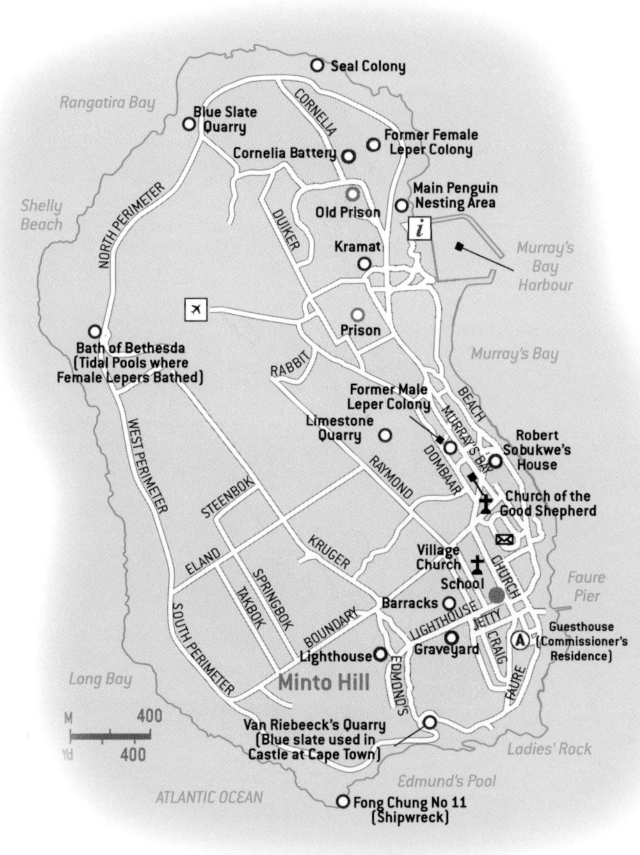
Seal Colony
Rangatira Bay
Blue Slate Quarry
CORNELIA
Former Female Leper Colony
Cornelia Battery
Shelly Beach
NORTH PERIMETER
DUIKER
Old Prison
Main Penguin Nesting Area
Kramat
Murray's Bay Harbour
Prison
Bath of Bethesda [Tidal Pools where Female Lepers Bathed]
RABBIT
Murray's Bay
Former Male Leper Colony
BEACH
Limestone Quarry
MURRAY'S BAY
DOMBAAR
Robert Sobukwe's House
WEST PERIMETER
RAYMOND
Church of the Good Shepherd
STEENBOK
KRUGER
Village Church
CHURCH
ELAND
SPRINGBOK
TAKBOK
School
Faure Pier
Barracks
BOUNDARY
LIGHTHOUSE
JETTY
CRAIG
Guesthouse [Commissioner's Residence]
SOUTH PERIMETER
Lighthouse
Graveyard
FAURE
EDMOND'S
Long Bay
Minto Hill
M 400
Yd 400
Van Riebeeck's Quarry [Blue slate used in Castle at Cape Town]
Ladies' Rock
Edmund's Pool
ATLANTIC OCEAN
Fong Chung No 11 [Shipwreck]

Lighthouse on Robben Island.

Milnerton & Ratanga Junction

Another gorgeous Cape day ends in Milnerton.

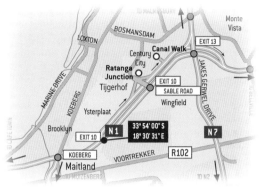

Stark, rocky and windswept, the West Coast has a unique beauty. Marine Drive (the M14) is a scenic route of dunes and sea that links Milnerton, Bloubergstrand and Melkbosstrand. Enjoy the best views of Table Mountain from Milnerton or Blouberg Beach.

CANAL WALK
Step into another world at Century City, sprawled alongside the N1 some 12km (7 miles) from the city centre. Built along a canal complete with rowboats, giant cupolas, painted murals and gilded columns decorate the malls – it's all a bit like the Wizard of Oz on 'E'. Upmarket shopping, a games arcade for the kids, a cinema complex and a fast food 'hall' and entertainment area will appease rumbling tums. A large stage and entertainment area adjoins the food hall, with dozens of TV sets to entertain patrons.

RATANGA JUNCTION (Note: Only open during peak seasons) The region's first full-scale theme park, Ratanga Junction will keep the kids out of your hair for hours. Launch them on 'jungle' cruises, or let them make like apes on the 18.5m (60ft) log-flume drop down Monkey Falls. If they have any nerves left, they can hit the pièce de résistance, the spine-chilling roller-coaster loops of the Cobra, which allow you to see the world at high speed – and from another perspective (upside down). Beware: ride queues can be LONG!

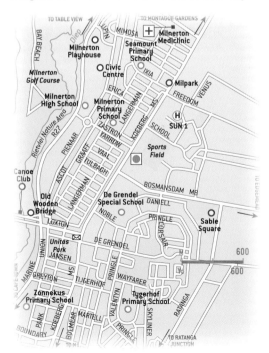

Canal Walk is flanked by a moat with boats for casual paddling after a heavy shopping trip!

On a rock pinnacle at one edge of Hout Bay beach is a statue of a leopard – a reminder of the sleek cats that once roamed the mountain slopes.

Camps Bay & Hout Bay

CAMPS BAY ▶

Cape Town's so-called Riviera – yes, France isn't the only country to have one – is where the rich people (and those who aspire to richness) play. It has palms, castor-sugar sands, pink sunsets, and is lined with terraced cafés and bars. They are the haunts of the scantily clad, sarong-enrobed young things in Gucci shades with mobile phones permanently attached to their ears. It's the place for bodacious curves and rippled, washboard stomachs. At sunset, trendoids hang out on the balcony of Blues Restaurant with something chilled in their hand to watch the sun sink behind the palm fronds, then move inside to try out the fusion cuisine served by eye-candy waitrons. If you're simply playing at being wealthy, find a secluded spot on the boulders at the beach and bid the sun farewell with your own bottle of sparkling wine.

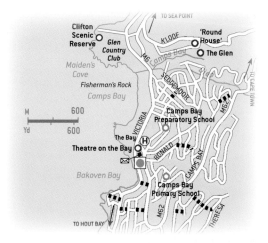

View of Lion's Head from Camps Bay beach.

Top Tip

In summer, Chapman's Peak Hotel is famous for its lobster, served as part of a giant mixed seafood platter and served on a balcony with great sea-views.

HOUT BAY ▼

If your yen is fish and chips eaten on unpretentious wooden benches with a harbour view, then Mariner's Wharf is for you (and the fish is so fresh you can almost taste the sea). This seafood bistro and fresh-fish market is built around Hout Bay's fishing harbour, with a beautifully placed curve of beach to the left and, to the right, a dockside for tourist cruises headed for Duiker Island to see the Cape fur seal colony. Work off your lunch with a stroll along the pretty beach where the mountains seem to rise from the sea; if it's late afternoon, you'll have to dodge the boisterous dogs taking their owners for a walk.

Cape fur seal.

23

Muizenberg & Kalk Bay

Beach huts on St James beach.

MUIZENBERG ◄

Lined by now-shabby façades of once-grand beach mansions, Muizenberg is best known for its 40km (25-mile) sweep of powder-sand cradling False Bay all the way to the Strand. Surfers learn about balance on its long rollers, swimmers love the 5°C difference in sea temperature from Clifton. Release the child in you; catch the train that snakes along the sea line from Muizenberg to Simon's Town and poke your head out the window to catch the wind in your face.

KALK BAY ▼

If the magpie in you can't resist bric-a-brac and glitter, they'll have to prise you away from the antique stores and art and craft shops lining Kalk Bay's main street. The Olympia Bakery will tempt you with the toasty, yeasty, crusty smells wafting out the door: it's so popular you have to chalk your name on the board and wait outside! Or lunch at Cape to Cuba, where trains thunder past while you're being served by pony-tailed waiters in berets.

Fishing boats in Kalk Bay's harbour.

1 Ou Kaapseweg
2 Boyes Drive
3 Main Road
4 Kommetjie-Noordhoek Main
5 Glencairn
6 Kommetjie Main
7 Chapman's Peak Drive

> **Top Tip**
> A drive (or run) along the winding Boyes Drive offers magnificent views of Muizenberg en route to Kalk Bay.

Penguins have an enviable libido and breed all year-round. A large appetite for pilchards and anchovies explains why they're busting out of their tuxedos.

Simon's Town & Boulders Beach

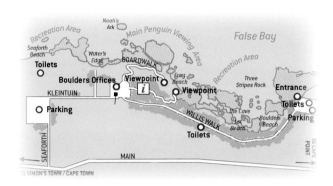

Penguins at Boulders Beach.

SIMON'S TOWN ▼

The Navy has been in Simon's Town's blood since the 1700s, and since 1957 it's been the South African naval base. If history's your bag, a guided historical tour from the rail station to the Martello Tower takes in, among others, a museum housed in The Residency (1777) – the town's oldest building, it features a World War II pub – the Warrior Toy Museum (boys will be boys), and the naval museum. A story to tug at your heartstrings is that of Just Nuisance, a Great Dane ship's mascot who so inveigled himself into British soldiers' hearts that he was formally enrolled in the Navy as an Able Seaman. He was given a full military funeral, wrapped in the White Ensign; 200 seamen attended. Don't miss his bronze statue in Jubilee Square, in the heart of the town.

BOULDERS ▲

Just past Simon's Town, at Boulders Beach, a family of African Penguins (formerly called "Jackass" Penguins) has moved in. There are now several thousand thanks to a bit of healthy breeding! Elevated boardwalks have been built so visitors can get up-close and personal, which you'll find yourself doing with childlike abandon. The penguins look back quizzically from every crevice, watching the world walk by.

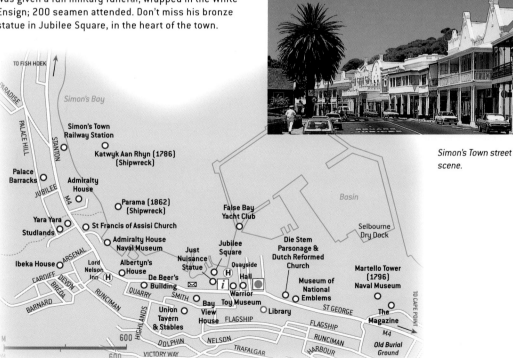

Simon's Town street scene.

Cape Winelands Driving Maps

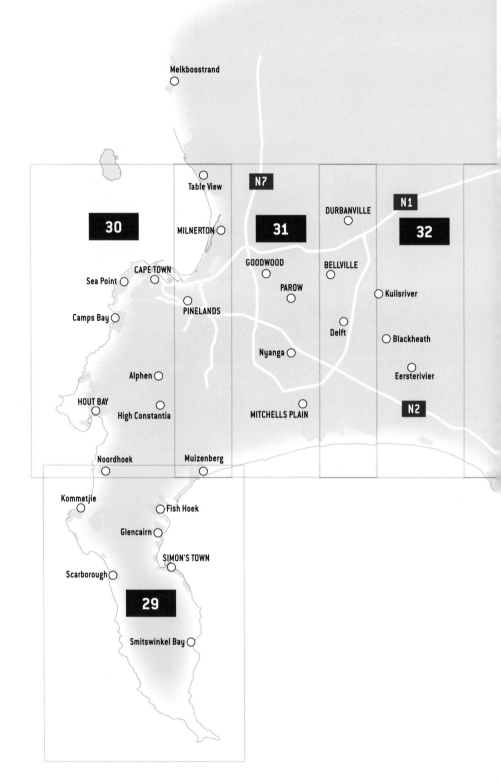

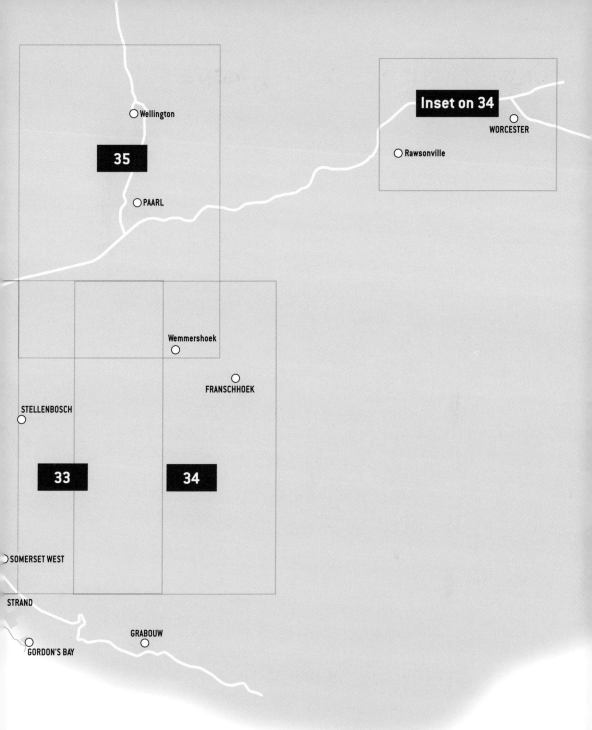

Wellington

35

PAARL

Inset on 34

WORCESTER

Rawsonville

Wemmershoek

FRANSCHHOEK

STELLENBOSCH

33

34

SOMERSET WEST

STRAND

GRABOUW

GORDON'S BAY

LEGEND

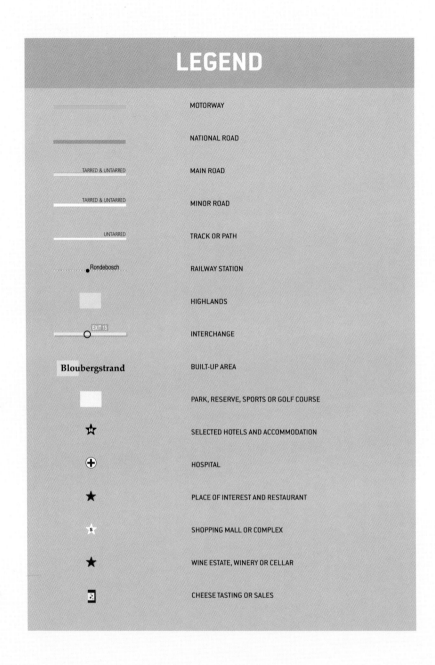

	MOTORWAY
	NATIONAL ROAD
TARRED & UNTARRED	MAIN ROAD
TARRED & UNTARRED	MINOR ROAD
UNTARRED	TRACK OR PATH
Rondebosch	RAILWAY STATION
	HIGHLANDS
EXIT 15	INTERCHANGE
Bloubergstrand	BUILT-UP AREA
	PARK, RESERVE, SPORTS OR GOLF COURSE
☆	SELECTED HOTELS AND ACCOMMODATION
⊕	HOSPITAL
★	PLACE OF INTEREST AND RESTAURANT
☆	SHOPPING MALL OR COMPLEX
★	WINE ESTATE, WINERY OR CELLAR
▣	CHEESE TASTING OR SALES

SCALE FOR ALL MAPS BETWEEN PAGES 28 & 35

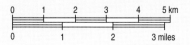

Chapman's
Bay
Viewpoint ★

30

★ WILD ROSE COUNTRY LODGE
★ SANDOLLAR GUEST HOUSE
Tunnel Cave

Kalk Bay Cave
Sayed Abdul   West Beach
Aziz's Kramat ●
Bailey's Cottage   Muizenberg
                    Neptune's
                    Corner

KALK BAY MOUNTAINS

Noordhoek Beach
Wreck of Kakapo (1900)
Klein Slangkop Point

Peers Cave ★
Clovelly
Country
Club   Clovelly

Rhodes Cottage
St James   Viewpoint
                Danger Beach
                St James

SUN VALLEY MALL
LONG BEACH MALL
SUN
VALLEY
Sunnydale

Fish
Hoek

Kalk Bay
Launch to Seal Island

THE LONG
BEACH
Kommetjie ★
Imhoffs Farm
Imhoffs Farmstall

Capri

2 Oceans Craft &
Culture Centre

THE AVENUE
Fish
Hoek

Clovelly
Fish
Hoek
Bay

Long Beach
Die Kom
Kommetjie Bay
Kommetjie
Lighthouse

Ocean
View

Glencairn
Heights

Sunny Cove ●

Soetwater

Da Gama
Park
Glencairn
JUST NUISANCE
SEASIDE INN ★

Old Glass ★
Works

Glencairn Beach
Elsies Bay
● Glencairn
Shelley Beach

Kleinplaas
Dam

Scratch Patch ★

★ Wreck of Clan Stuart (1917)

Mackerel Bay

Roman Rock ●

Witsand
Bay

Misty Cliffs

Red Hill

Long Beach
● Simon's Town
Bear Basics ★

SIMON'S TOWN
QUAYSIDE LODGE

Schuster's Bay

Camel Rock
Picnic Spot ★

Scarborough

Ibeka
LORD NELSON ★

The Magazine

Seaforth
The Boulders
● Penguin Colony

Schusterskraal ★
Picnic Spot

Jackson
Reservoir

Winford

Froggy Pond
Oatland Point

Table Mountain
National Park

Rawson
Reservoir

Froggy
Farm

Murdock Valley
Rocklands Point

Teeberg ★

Swartkopberge

Dassie Point
Miller's
Point
Koeël
Bay

Die Mond
Quicksands ★

The Fishery

Menskop Point

Olifantsbos Bay

Klaas Jagers

18° 27' 21" E
34° 15' 27" S

Danger Rock

Smitswinkel Bay
Viewpoint ★

Wreck of Thomas
T Tucker (1942) ★

THOMAS T. TUCKER
SHIPWRECK TRAIL

Batsata Rock ◌

Mast Bay

Batsata Cove

Old Cannon ★
Venus Pool

Wreck of Phyllisia (1968)

Hoek van Bobbejaan

Cape Point

Da Gama Monument (1497) ★
Buffels Bay

Blouberg Beach
Muishond Bay

Dias Cross (1488) ★

GOOD HOPE COASTAL WALK

Platboom Bay

Cape Point
Lighthouse

Viewpoint ★
Dias Beach ★
Cape
Point

Dias Cross ★
Cape of Good Hope

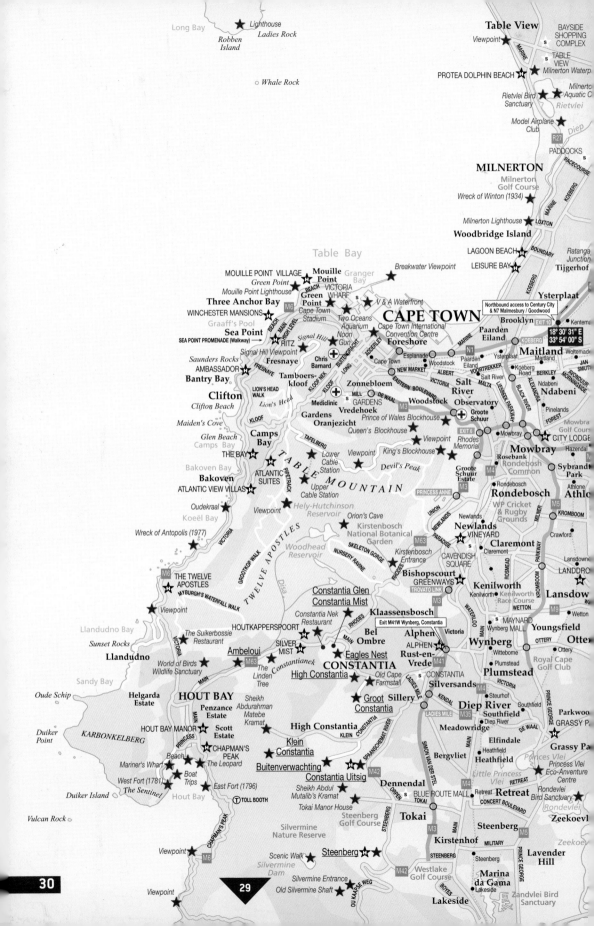

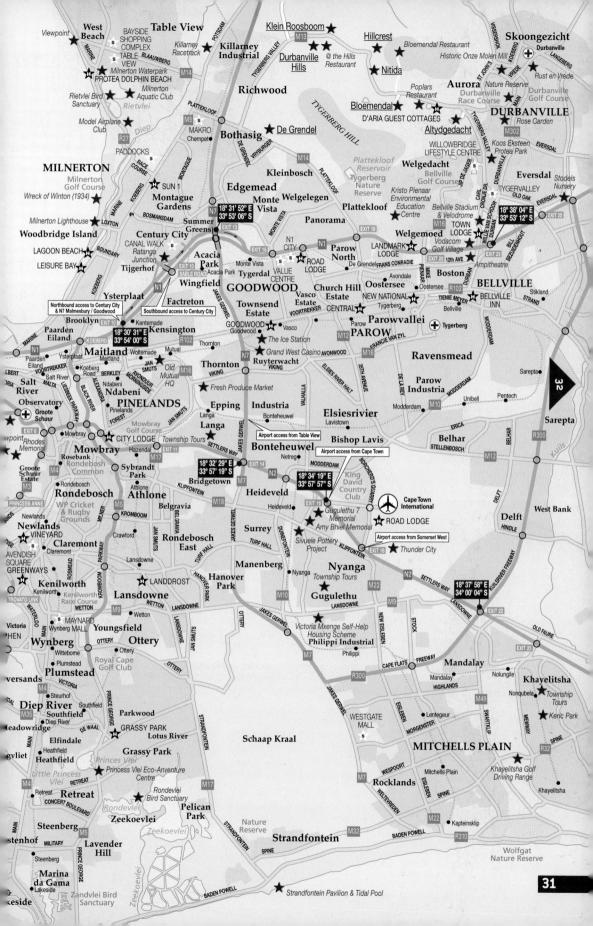

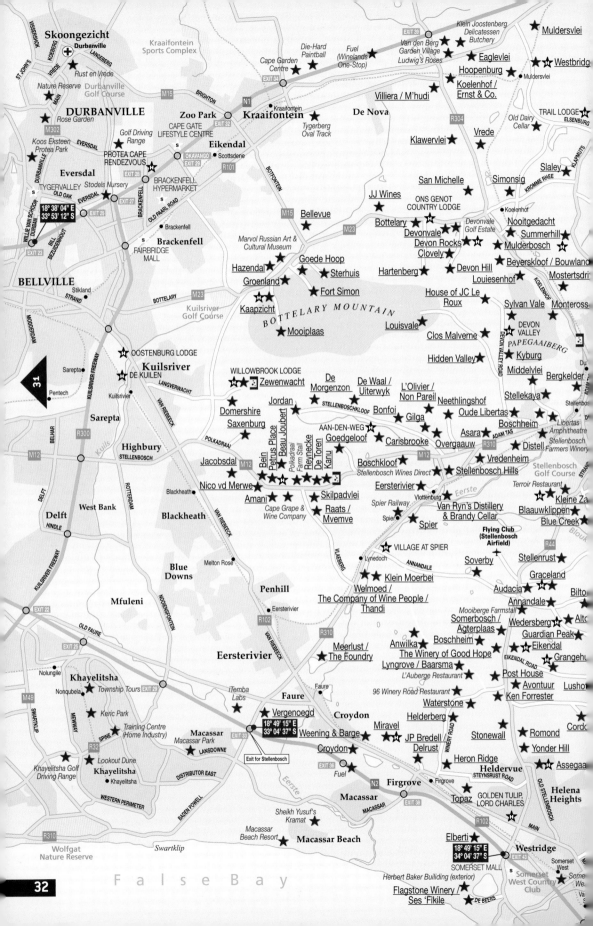

Skoongezicht
Durbanville
Kraaifontein Sports Complex
Cape Garden Centre
Die-Hard Paintball
Fuel (Winelands One-Stop)
Van den Berg Garden Village
Ludwig's Roses
Klein Joostenberg Delicatessen Butchery
Muldersvlei
Eaglevlei
Westbridge
Hoopenburg
Muldersvlei
Koelenhof / Ernst & Co.
Rust en Vrede
Nature Reserve
Durbanville Golf Course
DURBANVILLE
Rose Garden
Koos Eksteen Protea Park
Eversdal
Golf Driving Range
Zoo Park
CAPE GATE LIFESTYLE CENTRE
Kraaifontein
Tygerberg Oval Track
De Nova
Villiera / M'hudi
TRAIL LODGE ELSENBURG
Old Dairy Cellar
Vrede
Klawervlei
Slaley
Simonsig
San Michelle
JJ Wines
ONS GENOT COUNTRY LODGE
Koelenhof
Nooitgedacht
Summerhill
Mulderbosch
Beyerskloof / Bouwland
Mostertsdri
Devonvale Golf Estate
Devonvale
Devon Rocks
Clovely
Bottelary
Devon Hill
Louiesenhof
Hartenberg
Eikendal
Scottsdene
PROTEA CAPE RENDEZVOUS
Stodels Nursery
Old Oak
TYGERVALLEY
18° 38' 04" E
33° 53' 12" S
BRACKENFELL HYPERMARKET
Brackenfell
FAIRBRIDGE MALL
BELLVILLE
Stikland
Marvol Russian Art & Cultural Museum
Hazendal
Groenland
Goede Hoop
Sterhuis
Fort Simon
House of JC Le Roux
Sylvan Vale
Monteross
DEVON VALLEY
PAPEGAAIBERG
Kaapzicht
BOTTELARY MOUNTAIN
Louisvale
Clos Malverne
Hidden Valley
Kyburg
Bergkelder
Mooiplaas
Middelvlei
Stellekaya
Kuilsriver Golf Course
OOSTENBURG LODGE
Kuilsriver
DE KUILEN
Sarepta
Pentech
WILLOWBROOK LODGE
Zewenwacht
De Morgenzon
De Waal / Uiterwyk
L'Olivier / Non Pareil
Neethlingshof
Libertas Amphitheatre
Boschheim
Stellenbosch Farmers' Winery
Distell
Sarepta
Highbury
Jordan
Bonfoi
Gilga
Oude Libertas
Domershire
Saxenburg
Beau Joubert
Petrus Place
Polkadraai Farm Stall
Reynecke
De Toren
Kanu
AAN-DEN-WEG
Goedgeloof
Carisbrooke
Asara
Overgaauw
Bein
Jacobsdal
Stellenbosch
Boschkloof
Vredenheim
Stellenbosch Hills
Stellenbosch Golf Course
Nico vd Merwe
Amani
Blackheath
Cape Grape & Wine Company
Skilpadvlei
Raats / Mvemve
Eersterivier
Van Ryn's Distillery & Brandy Cellar
Terroir Restaurant
Kleine Za
Spier Railway
Vlottenburg
Spier
Blaauwklippen
Blue Creek
Melton Rose
West Bank
Delft
Blue Downs
Penhill
Eersterivier
VILLAGE AT SPIER
Lynedoch
Flying Club (Stellenbosch Airfield)
Soverby
Stellenrust
Klein Moerbei
Graceland
Welmoed / The Company of Wine People / Thandi
Audacia
Bilto
Annandale
Mooiberge Farmstall
Somerbosch / Agterplaas
Wedersberg
Alto
Mfuleni
Anwilka
Boschheim
Guardian Peak
Eikendal
Grangehu
EIKENDAL ROAD
Meerlust / The Foundry
The Winery of Good Hope
Lyngrove / Baarsma
Post House
Lusho
Avontuur
Ken Forrester
Eersterivier
96 Winery Road Restaurant
L'Auberge Restaurant
Waterstone
Vergenoegd
18° 49' 15" E
33° 04' 37" S
Croydon
Weening & Barge
Miravel
JP Bredell
Delrust
Helderberg
Stonewall
Romond
Yonder Hill
Assegaa
Macassar
Macassar Park
LANSDOWNE
Croydon
Fuel
Firgrove
Heron Ridge
Heldervue
STEYNSRUST ROAD
Cordo
Khayelitsha
Township Tours
Nonqubela
Nolungile
iTemba Labs
Faure
Macassar
Topaz
GOLDEN TULIP, LORD CHARLES
Helena Heights
Keric Park
Training Centre (Home Industry)
Lookout Dune
Khayelitsha Golf Driving Range
Khayelitsha
Elberti
18° 49' 15" E
34° 04' 37" S
Westridge
SOMERSET MALL
Somerset West Country Club
Sheikh Yusuf's Kramat
Macassar Beach Resort
Macassar Beach
Herbert Baker Building (exterior)
Flagstone Winery / Ses 'Fikile
DE BEERS
Wolfgat Nature Reserve
Swartklip

Klein Joostenberg
Delicatessen
Butchery

★★ Muldersvlei

★ Avonvrede
★ Mont Destin
★ Niel
★ Joubert
★ Babylons Toren

Safariland Game Park

Ludwig's Roses
★ Eaglevlei
Hoopenburg
Koelenhof / Ernst & Co.

★★ Westbridge
☆ Mitre's Edge
Le Bonheur
• Muldersvlei
Warwick

★ Marianne
☆ Natte Valleij
Backsberg
Maze

★ Cowlin
★ Noble Hill
• Simondium

★ Dawn Mountains

Pearl Valley Jack
Nicklaus Signature Golf
Course & Spa

★★ Zonneblom

Groot Drakenstein
Cultural Centre

Victor Verster

R304
★ Vrede
★ Klawervlei

★★ Marklew
★ Lievland
Laibach
TRAIL LODGE
ELSENBURG
Old Dairy Cellar
☆ Delvera (Wine tasting, restaurant & shop)

Wiesenhof Game Park

★ Rupert & Rothchild Vigneroñs
Drakensig / Marais Viljoen

★ Plaisir de Merle
☆ Vrede en Lust

☆ The Spotted Giraffe Crafts & Curios

SIMONDIUM'S COUNTRY LODGE
LEKKER WIJN GUEST HOUSE
☆ Allée Bleue
Café Allée Bleue
★ Solms-Delta

★★ San Michelle
Simonsig
Slaley

★ Uitkyk
Kanonkop
★ Delheim

S I M O N S B E R G

Groot Drakenstein •
Boschendal Manor House (1865)
★ Boschendal
Bandstand
L'Ormarins / Anthonij Rupert

R45

Devonvale
Devonvale Golf Estate
• Koelenhof
Nooitgedacht
Summerhill
★ Mulderbosch
☆ L'Avenir

★ Quion Rock
★ Muratie
☆ KNORHOEK GUESTHOUSES
★ Remhoogte
Knorhoek

★ Normandy

Devon Rocks
★ Devon Hill
Louiesenhof
Beyerskloof / Bouwland
Mostertsdrift
R44

★ Morgenhof

THE HYDRO AT STELLENBOSCH
★ Thelema Mountain
Tokara
Alluvia
La Pommier
★ Zorgvliet
Vuurberg

Pniel

House of JC Le Roux
Sylvan Vale
☆ DEVON VALLEY
Monterosso
Simonsberg

★ Re Mogo
Sentinel Vinyards
Rustenberg

R310

os Malverne
dden Valley
PAPEGAAIBERG
DEVON VALLEY ROAD
Kyburg
Middelvlei
Bergkelder
Research Farm
Nietvoorbij
Du Toit
HELSHOOGTE
CSIR

Idas Valley Dam
The Olive Shed
BENVENUTO
HELSHOOGTE PASS
Delaire

Hillcrest Berry Orchards
★ Molen Vliet
Kylemore
★ Camberley

Neethlingshof
Stellekaya
Oude Libertas
Vilafonté
• Stellenbosch
DORP
★ Anatu
Lanzerac
LELIE
BIRD
MERRIMAN
MARTINSON
AUBERGE ROZENDAL
☆ Rozendal
LANZERAC MANOR

★ Bartinney
★ Clouds
★ Rainbows End

Asara
Boschheim
ADAM TAS
Distell
R310
Overgaauw
Libertas Amphitheatre
Stellenbosch Farmers Winery
★ The High Road
STELLENBOSCH
Constellation
★ Klein Gustrouw

☆ Le Riche
★ Neil Ellis / Stark-Condé / Meyer-Näkel

JONKERSHOEK MOUNTAINS

Vredenheim
★ Stellenbosch Hills
lottenburg
Eerste
Stellenbosch Golf Course
Terroir Restaurant
STRAND
PARADYSKLOOF

Kierie Kwaak
☆ Jonkershoek
★ Jonkershoek Tea Garden
JONKERSHOEK

Kleinplaas Dam
Jonkershoek

Van Ryn's Distillery & Brandy Cellar
Flying Club (Stellenbosch Airfield)
R44
☆ Kleine Zalze
Blaauwklippen
Blue Creek
BLOUKLIP
★ Vriesenhof
★ Cape Hutton
Klein Das Bosch

STELLENBOSCH MOUNTAINS

BOLAND TRAIL
JONKERSHOEK STATE FOREST PANORAMA CIRCUIT

Soverby
Stellenrust
Graceland
Audacia
Stellenzicht
Waterford
Rust en Rede
★ Dornier Wines
★ Kleinmond
BLAAUWKLIPPEN
★ Keermont

Assegaaibosch Nature Reserve

Jonkershoek Nature Reserve

JONKERSHOEK STATE FOREST PANORAMA CIRCUIT

Mooiberge Farmstall
Somerbosch / Agterplaas
oschheim
ngrove / Baarsma
Auberge restaurant
Annandale
☆ Wedersberg
Guardian Peak
Eikendal
Grangehurst
Bilton
Alto
Haskell
★ Ernie Els
Uva Mira Vyds
ANNANDALE
Dombeya Yarns Farm
EIKENDAL ROAD
Longridge
Hidden Valley
De Trafford / Sijnn

Hottentots Holland Nature Reserve

Post House
Avontuur
Lushof
★ Con Spirare
Ken Forrester
Waterstone
★ Helderberg
WINERY ROAD
Stonewall
★ Romond
Cordoba

H E L D E R B E R G

Heron Ridge
★ Yonder Hill
☆☆ Assegaai
Heldervue
STEYNSRUST ROAD
Helderberg Nature Reserve
☆ Erinvale

BOLAND TRAIL

Topaz
GOLDEN TULIP, LORD CHARLES
Helena Heights
OLD STELLENBOSCH ROAD

Lourens

R102
Elberti ★
18° 49' 15" E
34° 04' 37" S
Westridge
EXIT 43
MAIN
SOMERSET WEST
★ Kings Kloof
★ Lourensford

SOMERSET MALL
agstone Winery / Ses 'Fikile
DE BEERS
s
Somerset West Country Club
Somerset West
VICTORIA
Van der Stel
LOURENSFORD
MAIN
D'Vine Restaurant
★★ Hathersage
Lourens River Bridge
★ Morgenster
★ Vergelegen
★★ Morgenster Olive Grove
★ Wedderville

35

34

33

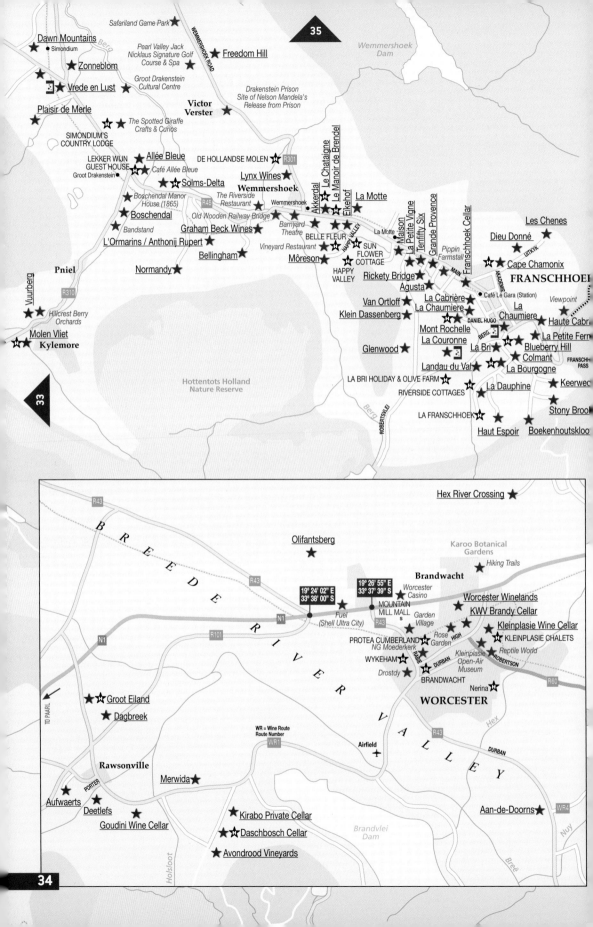

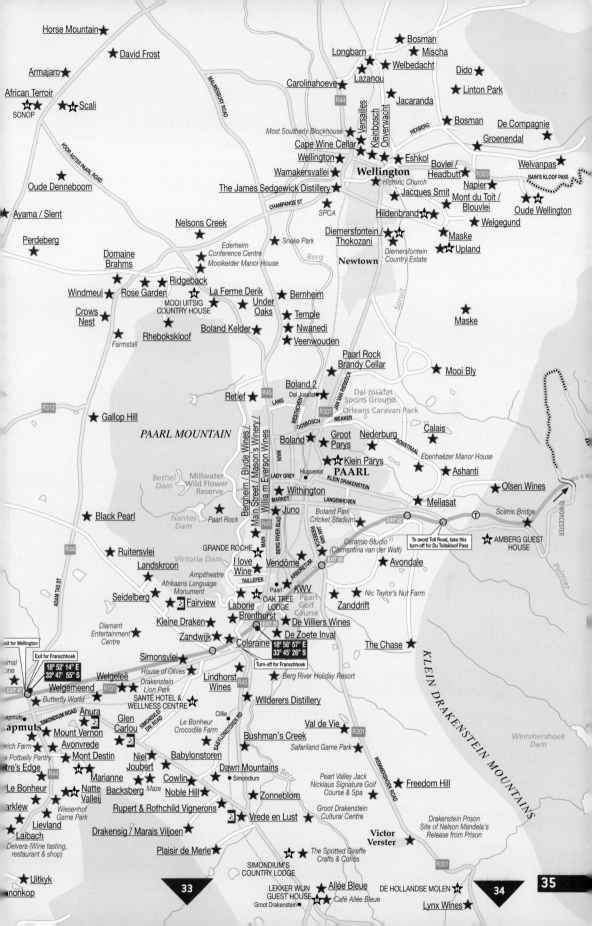

Horse Mountain ★

David Frost ★

Armajaro ★

African Terroir ☆☆ ☆★ Scali
SONOP

Oude Denneboom ★

Ayama / Slent ★

Perdeberg ★

Domaine Brahms ★

Windmeul ★ Rose Garden ★ Ridgeback ★
☆ La Ferme Derik ★
MOOI UITSIG COUNTRY HOUSE

Crows Nest ★

Rhebokskloof ★
Farmstall

Boland Kelder ★

Gallop Hill ★

PAARL MOUNTAIN

Black Pearl ★

Ruitersvlei ★

Landskroon ★

Seidelberg ★

Diamant Entertainment Centre

Kleine Draken ★

Zandwijk ★

Simonsvlei ★
House of Olives ★

Welgeleë ★

Welgemeend ★
Butterfly World
R101
Exit for Wellington

Exit for Franschhoek
18° 52' 14" E
33° 47' 55" S
EXIT 47

Anura ★
Mount Vernon ★
Avonrede ★
Mont Destin ★

Glen Carlou ★

Niel Joubert ★

Marianne ★
Natte Valleij ★

Backsberg ★
Maze

Cowlin ★
Noble Hill ★

Babylonstoren ★

Dawn Mountains ★
● Simondium

Le Bonheur ★
Wiesenhof Game Park

Lievland ★

Laibach ★
Delvera (Wine tasting, restaurant & shop)

Uitkyk ★
Kanonkop

Horse Mountain ★

Bosman ★
Longbarn ★ Mischa ★
Welbedacht ★
Carolinahoeve ★ Lazanou ★ Dido ★
Versailles Linton Park ★
Kleinbosch Jacaranda ★
Most Southerly Blockhouse ★ Onverwacht Bosman ★ De Compagnie ★
Cape Wine Cellar ★ Eshkol ★ Groenendal ★
Wellington ★ ★ Bovlei / Welvanpas ★
Wamakersvallei ★ ★ Wellington Headbutt BAIN'S KLOOF PASS
HEXBERG Napier ★
The James Sedgewick Distillery ★ Historic Church Jacques Smit ★ Mont du Toit / ☆ Oude Wellington
CHAMPANGE ST SPCA Hildenbrand ★ Blouvlei ★ Welgegund
☆ Maske ★
Nelsons Creek ★ Ederheim Diemersfontein / ☆☆ Upland ★
Conference Centre Thokozani
Mooikelder Manor House Newtown Diemersfontein
Snake Park ★ Country Estate

Berg

Bernheim ★
Under Oaks ★
Temple ★ Maske ★
Nwanedi ★
Veenwouden ★

Spruit

Paarl Rock Brandy Cellar ★
Mooi Bly ★

Boland 2 ★
Retief ★ Dal Josafat Dal Josafat Sports Ground
R45 LANG Orleans Caravan Park
WESTHOVEN MEAKER Calais ★
R301 Nederburg ★
OOSBOSCH Groot Boland ★ Parys ★
Ebenhaëzer Manor House
Klein Parys ☆★ Ashanti ★
PAARL Olsen Wines ★
LADY GREY Huguenot ● Mellasat ★ Scenic Bridge
Withington ★ KLEIN DRAKENSTEIN T
MARKET LANGENHOVEN Boland Park EXIT 62 AMBERG GUEST
Juno ★ Cricket Stadium To avoid Toll Road, take this ☆ HOUSE
R45 turn-off for Du Toitskloof Pass
GRANDE ROCHE Ceramic Studio
Nantes Paarl Rock EXIT 59 (Clementina van der Walt)
Dam I love ☆ Avondale ★
Victoria Dam Wine ★ Vendôme ★ ARBORETUM
Ampitheatre TAILLEFER Paarl ● Nic Taylor's Nut Farm
Afrikaans Language KWV ★
Monument Fairview ☆★ OAK TREE Paarl The Chase ★
Laborie ★ LODGE Golf Zanddrift ★
Brenthurst ★ EXIT 58 Course
De Villiers Wines ★
Coleraine ★ 18° 58' 57" E
33° 45' 26" S De Zoete Inval ★
Turn-off for Franschhoek
Berg River Holiday Resort ●

Drakenstein
Lion Park
Lindhorst
Wines ★ Wilderers Distillery ★
SANTÉ HOTEL &
WELLNESS CENTRE Val de Vie ★
Cillie R301
Le Bonheur Bushman's Creek ★
Crocodile Farm Safariland Game Park ●
Pearl Valley Jack
Zonneblom ★ Nicklaus Signature Golf Freedom Hill ★
Course & Spa
Rupert & Rothchild Vignerons ★ Groot Drakenstein
Cultural Centre
Vrede en Lust ★ Drakenstein Prison
Victor Site of Nelson Mandela's
Verster Release from Prison
Drakensig / Marais Viljoen ★
Plaisir de Merle ★ The Spotted Giraffe
☆ ★ Crafts & Curios
SIMONDIUM'S
COUNTRY LODGE
LEKKER WIJN ★ Allée Bleue DE HOLLANDSE MOLEN ☆
GUEST HOUSE ☆ Lynx Wines ★
Groot Drakenstein ● Café Allée Bleue

R312

ADAM TAS ST

R44

KLEIN DRAKENSTEIN MOUNTAINS

TO WORCESTER

Palmiet

Wemmershoek Dam

WEMMERSHOEK ROAD

MALMESBURY ROAD

VOOR AGTER PAARL ROAD

BERG RIVER BLVD

MAIN

JAN VAN RIEBEECK

SONSTRAAL

Bergheim / Blyde Wines /
Main Street / Mason's Winery /
Willia m Everson Wines

Bethel Dam

Millwater
Wild Flower
Reserve

SIMONSVLEI
DIV ROAD

BABYLONSTOREN RD

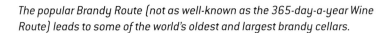

The Cape Winelands: Constantia

It's this part of the Western Cape Province that brings out the superlatives. How do you compete with towering jagged mountains, one range giving way to another, and many carrying whimsical names like Hex ('witch'), Drakenstein ('dragon stone') and Riviersonderend ('river with no end')? At their foot are tightly manicured vine terraces – and to cap it all, the eternally graceful curved and moulded gables of historical manor houses, a heritage left behind by early Dutch settlers. Passes forged through this mountain barrier to the east made it a gateway to the rest of the country. A region that, early on, was baptised the 'overberg', meaning 'over (or across) the mountains'. The Western Cape's winelands are the main reason for South Africa's plum position as seventh-largest wine producer in the world. A constantly mushrooming number of estates presently stand in the 90s; there are just fewer than 70 co-operatives and over 100 private cellars. The wineland areas are accessed via two major national routes, the N1 and N2, with multiple connecting and well-signposted principal roads. Crossing the mountains to the Overberg – and the 'southern' Cape region – the seaside summer 'play-zone' of Hermanus is king of whale-watching capitals. It has succeeded in turning Whale Season into a major festival.

CONSTANTIA ▶

The official Constantia Wine Route is limited to five estates – but dynamite comes in small packages! You will succumb to leafy oaks, whitewashed gables, vine-terraces and soaring mountains so close you could touch them (well, almost). Buitenverwachting, Groot

Left: Farm workers pluck truckloads of grapes from the vast vineyard estates.
Bottom: Vines, clear skies and mountain ranges stretch as far as the eye can see ...

Constantia, Klein Constantia and Constantia Uitsig all formed (at one time) part of a farm granted to Simon van der Stel in 1685. Groot Constantia offers the most bang for your buck in historic terms, with its old coach house, the Cloete wine cellar (now a wine museum), the manor house (converted into a 17th-century museum) and the Jonkershuis, now a restaurant. If, like Bacchus, you're into nectar of the gods, nearby Klein Constantia still produces Vin de Constance, a sweet wine from Muscat de Frontignac (get your tongue around that one!). Still made in the 18th-century tradition, this wine has seduced the taste buds of Napoleon, Bismarck and even Jane Austen. In the neighbourhood, Steenberg Estate (visits by appointment!) is also producing some memorable fermented juice from the vine.

Durbanville

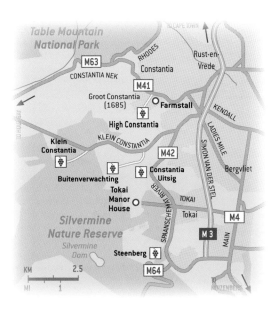

DURBANVILLE WINE ROUTE ▼

Durbanville is the upper crust (read: monied) residential and shopping mecca of Cape Town's Northern Suburbs – and settled into undulating hills and mountains, it puts on a pretty face, too. With the surrounding slopes clothed in vines, these are producing very respectable grapes that are being pressed in turn into highly quaffable wines. Durbanville Hills winery waves its magic wand with some very fine lemon-butter chardonnays and grassy-nosed sauvignon blancs ('sav blanc' and 'chard' to the wine toff). Diemersdal, Nitida, Meerendal and Altydgedacht don't do too badly either on all lip-smacking scores – red and white.

Top Right: The slave bell at Altydgedacht wine estate, on the Durbanville Wine Route.
Below: Buitenverwachting homestead looks out across a sea of vines.

Above: Groot Constantia's triangle gable.

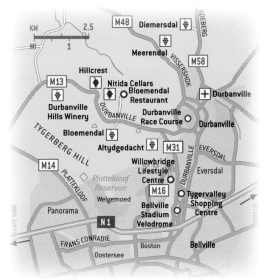

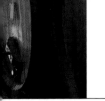

Oom Samie se Winkel is an old-fashioned village store crammed with collectables, artefacts of bygone years, chunky preserves and basketry.

Stellenbosch

SEAT OF LEARNING

Its streets lined with leafy oaks, this pretty university town's buildings rub shoulders with historical cottages and restored Cape Dutch, Cape Georgian, Regency and Victorian houses. Dorp Street is a marvel for its meticulously preserved façades, lined up like toy soldiers, and most of them historical monuments. You'll have built up a thirst from walking – Dorp is a l-o-o-o-n-g street – so it'll be necessary to make a dent on the students' famous local, De Akker. Stellenbosch also buys into café society, and there's a good selection of trendy coffee shops spilling out onto the pavement. If this is all too lowbrow for you, the university town has some good art galleries and art museums: Dorp Street Gallery, the gallery at 34 Ryneveld Street and the Rembrandt van Rijn Art Gallery.

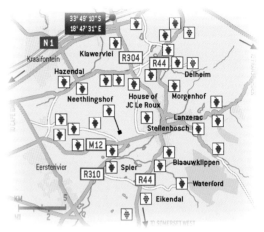

Oom Samie se winkel: Time-Warp City.

GETTING SLOSHED IN STELLENBOSCH

You can only visit three or four cellars in a day before you completely fall over, let alone follow the white lines on the road. You also obviously need to build in time to stop for lunch. At last count there were around 30 cellars and co-ops on four major roads within a 12km (7-mile) radius from Cape Town, so choose wisely. Delheim has atmosphere: low-lit, brick-arched wine cellar with wooden tables and benches; Morgenhof has a formal French-style garden and a tasting room with floor-to-ceiling views; Blaauwklippen is a working farm with vintage coaches, carriages and offering a coachman's platter for lunch.

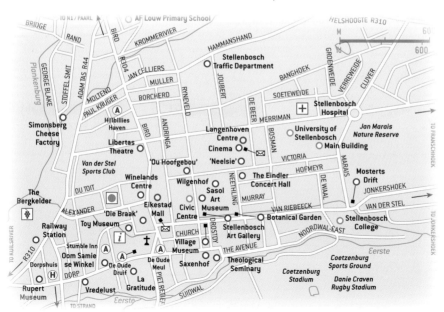

Cabrière's Achim von Arnim will utterly charm you as he deftly lops off the necks of Pierre Jourdan wine bottles with a sabre (sabrage in French).

Franschhoek

Late afternoon winter vineyards, snow-capped mountain peaks … it's red wine time.

Franschhoek is a den for hedonists. Here you can party-party! Taking its cue from the French, it's a centre for wining and dining, festivals and fun. Year-round, the town stages festivals celebrating olives, cheese, grapes … and the cherry on top is Bastille Day. For wine farms to visit, the graciously gabled L'Ormarins overlooks an ornamental pond and has a low, wooden-beam-ceilinged tasting room; La Motte's medieval-like long table and high-backed chairs look through glass panelling onto an oak-barrelled maturation cellar; Môreson, part of a working farm, has a large airy restaurant and a pretty terrace; and Haute Provence gives you superb wines in utterly gracious surrounds.

> **Top Tip**
> *Sip chilled wine on the lawns at La Petite Ferme and take in the most stupendous view; then move onto the terrace for their smoked trout with horseradish sauce.*

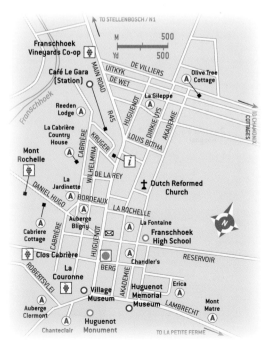

Franschhoek Vineyards Co-op.

Paarl

The Taal Monument will get tongues wagging.

The Main Street in Paarl, which tails the Berg River, runs an amazing 11km (7 miles) and boasts rows of 18th- and 19th-century Cape Dutch and Georgian houses. About one-fifth of the country's total wine production comes from Paarl, and the most striking symbol of its wine history is La Concorde, a Neo-Classical building with a sculpted pediment, dating back to 1956.

Don't make any detours round Fairview Wine Estate with its lip-smacking wines at lip-smacking prices. Watch the farm's Saanen (Swiss) goats nimbly navigating a thin spiral ramp up a tall tower, and then test their milk cheeses, some rolled in herbs or black pepper ... but the garlic cheese stand apart! At Zanddrift you can taste wines in a stone chapel that was built in the early 1940s by Italian prisoners of war. Nederburg, whose exquisite manor house has been captured by the click of many a camera lens, is internationally famous for its annual wine auction, and its auctioneer, Brit Patrick Grubb.

The swooping white spires on the hill are part of the Taal (or 'language') Monument, a tribute to the Afrikaans taal, it has three domes and three small pillars that vary in size and height. Nearby, Paarl Mountain can be climbed with the help of chain handholds. This granite outcrop, the world's second largest after Australia's Uluru, wears its age well – 500 million years and counting.

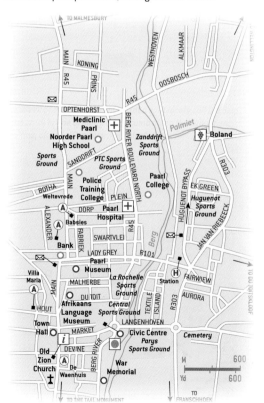

Paarl Rock, second in size only to Ayers Rock.

Wellington is known for its fresh-pressed olive oil (grown in the area), tanning industry and leather products (shoes, belts, handbags ... even couches!).

Wellington

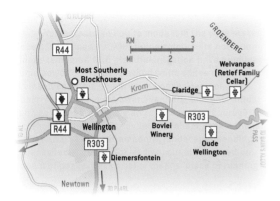

Green bottles waiting for wine at Welgegund estate in Wellington.

WELLINGTON

Wellington is the headquarters of South Africa's dried fruit industry – you must taste the mebos, a sour-sweet chewy-fruity taste explosion. Inevitably, it's always the wine that draws the bees to the honey ... although Wellington still has to prove itself in the elegant wine stakes due to its dry, sunbaked climate. It also has its share of manor houses, among them Twistniet, the original homestead around which the town was built. The greatest stir is caused by Bain's Kloof Pass (northeast of the town via the R303 highway), 30km (19 miles) of spectacular rock, sky and views.

After the picnic spot at the summit, the pass drops to the Breede River valley where ravines, waterfalls and dramatic rock formations are your travel companions. Take your hat off to the pass builders, Andrew Geddes Bain and his son, Thomas. The interior, beyond these craggy mountains, was virtually impassable before the Bains arrived armed with their pickaxes. In winter, the peaks flanking Wellington often slap on their pretty snow-dusted aprons.

On Wednesdays and Saturdays a steam train leaves Cape Town at 9:30am, stopping at Spier (it has its own station), and returning in the afternoon.

Classic Wine Estates

GROOT CONSTANTIA ▶

The manor house (1685) is today a museum of authentic 17th-century life filled with paintings, furniture and objets d'art. On its gable (sculpted by Anton Anreith) rests the figure of Abundance, a more recent addition. If all this history is way too much for you, the Cloete wine cellar holds some gorgeous old drinking vessels and implements of torture once used for winemaking. No-one said touring was easy, so rest up in the Jonkershuis to sample traditional Cape Malay fare. 'Jonker' was used to describe an estate owner's elder, bachelor son who generally had his own house on the estate. You can also choose to picnic under 300-year-old oak, chestnut, olive and banana trees.

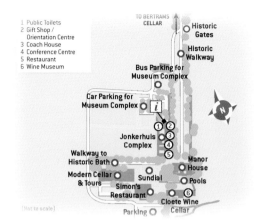

1 Public Toilets
2 Gift Shop / Orientation Centre
3 Coach House
4 Conference Centre
5 Restaurant
6 Wine Museum

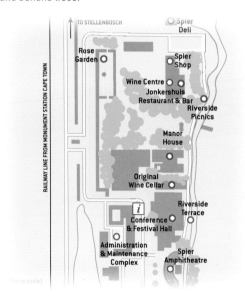

stomach, if you haven't yet tired of Eastern influences, the tables at the Jonkershuis groan delectably under the weight of an Indonesian and Cape Malay buffet.

BOSCHENDAL ▼

The ace in this estate's pack of cards is its H-shaped manor house, built in 1812 in the graceful Flemish style. Authentically furnished, from its cow-dung-washed kitchen floor to its wooden-beamed rafters, it's crammed with 18th-century treasures. One of the rooms holds a Dutch long-case clock (made in 1748) whose face shows the date, day of the week, moon phases, month and appropriate zodiac sign ... as well as the tide in Amsterdam! And then there's the ubiquitous restaurant offering traditional Cape fare – the buffet here is the gossip of the winelands. Equally whispered about are the picnic lunches on lawns shaded by pine trees, whose focal point is a lily pond beside the latticework of a pretty Victorian gazebo. Oh ... wine tasting in the taphuis or under the oaks is also pretty fine!

> **Top Tip**
> Purr with the cuddly young cheetahs found in enclosures on Spier's estate. Part of a controlled breeding programme, all funds go towards the Cheetah Conservation Fund.

SPIER ▲

There are no flies on this impressive complex that sprawls alongside the Eerste River: a wine farm, three restaurants, a wine shop and a delicatessen / farm stall adjoining pretty picnic grounds lying around a lake and decorated with canvas umbrellas and wooden benches. That's not all: an impressive open-air theatre has hosted an extensive repertoire of dance, theatre, jazz, classical concerts ... and even opera. You can't miss it – it's presided over by gilded life-size statues of the Muses. Classical Greece comes to Wine Country. On matters of the

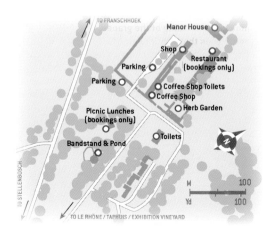

Somerset West

View of homestead and trees at Vergelegen Wine Estate.

SOMERSET WEST

In front of Vergelegen's manor house stand five old camphor trees that were planted in 1700 by the Cape governor, Willem Adriaan van der Stel. This large town lies to the south of the Stellenbosch winelands and has False Bay as one neighbour and the rugged Hottentots Holland mountains – the route to the Overberg – as another. The pride of the area is the Vergelegen Wine Estate ... and its ochre-walled, thatched and gabled manor home once belonged to a different Van der Stel. Willem Adriaan's claim to fame? He was demoted by the Dutch East India Co. for unfettered spending and incompetence, and deftly removed from his post.

DRINKING OF THE VINE

Vergelegen has a unique, gravity-fed underground cellar – grapes are fed into destalking, crushing and steel maturation tanks from above ground, thus maximising the effects of gravity and minimising bruising of the grapes. The theory goes that gentler grape handling produces smoother, rounder wines ... so the tree-huggers may well have a point, after all! If it's tea you're after (not wine!), the flower-bedecked Lady Phillips Tea Garden will wrap you round its pretty little finger. The garden was named in honour of Lord and Lady Phillips, who lived here from 1917 to 1940.

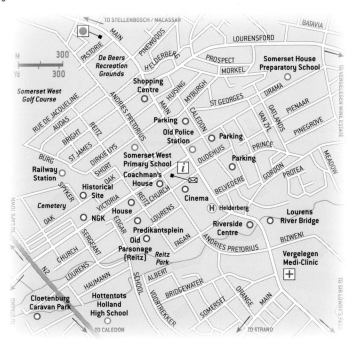

Strand & Gordon's Bay

Casting a line into the ocean at dusk proves popular with locals and tourists.

STRAND ▼

Strand ('beach' in Dutch and Afrikaans) is a modern town lying just south of Somerset West, on the furthest extent of False Bay's shores. From here swathes of white sand, like the broad blade of a scythe, curve all the way to Muizenberg, with the R310 running almost parallel to the coastline. The Strand promenade and restaurant jut out into the ocean, and beaches are packed in the holiday seasons (mental picture: sardines in a tin!).

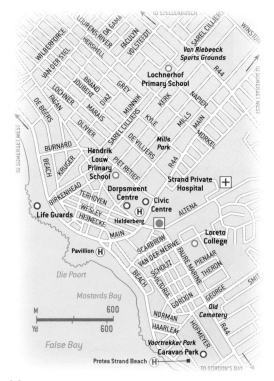

GORDON'S BAY ▶

Once a simple fishing harbour, Gordon's Bay has grown up. Now a very fine yacht club is flanked by swish holiday apartments and seaside homes, and the bay looks like some Mediterranean resort with the constant to-ing and fro-ing of glam yachts, motorboats and (not-so-glam) fishing vessels. If you're in luck and the shoals are running, you can charter a deep-sea boat to test your mettle with tunny and yellowtail. Bikini Beach has been earmarked for sunworshipping (what did you think?), while Main Beach is marked by testosterone – it's the active watersports zone of coloured sails, shrieking laughter, spraying water and the racket of twin-horsepower engines.

Clarence Drive offers delightful views and secretive coves.

> **Top Tip**
> Clarence Drive (from Gordon's Bay) tightly snakes its way between the coastline and the stony Hottentots Holland slopes all the way to Pringle Bay, and almost within spitting distance of the heaving seas. Dare we say … it rivals Chapman's Peak!

JONKERSHOEK AND HOTTENTOTS HOLLAND ▶

The rough and rugged mountains of Stellenbosch, Somerset West and Gordon's Bay allow hikers and nature lovers to dust off technology and big-city pressures. To the east of Stellenbosch, sandwiched between the town and Jonkershoek mountains lies the Jonkershoek valley. Part of the Jonkershoek State Forest, walkers can hike through dense wooded forests and swim in crystal streams running over pebbled riverbeds. Idyllic? There are high waterfalls, wildflowers in summer, and mountain birds to spot – including Black Eagle, Peregrine Falcon and Mountain Buzzard. If you're into trees, you can identify the highly protected hardwood species – yellowwood, stinkwood and ironwood – that are not quite fully depleted by the early settlers who loved their fine-grained timber (and which proved perfect for the finest Cape furniture).

If you've got a good eye for unusual fynbos species, keep them peeled for the rare marsh rose and the blushing bride.

Strand & Gordon's Bay

Further to the east is the Hottentots Holland Nature Reserve covering an area of 400ha (988 acres) — challenging terrain for walkers who've progressed beyond baby steps and are ready for the real world. Cars have to stay behind, as this is serious hiking: backpacks with sleeping gear and food and cooking utensils. The Boland Trail runs through the reserve, a three-day, 41km (25-mile) route through fynbos, across stony hills and along goose-bump-chilly mountain pools. The trail has also been downsized into shorter, circular sections for those not quite ready to rough it under the stars for two nights.

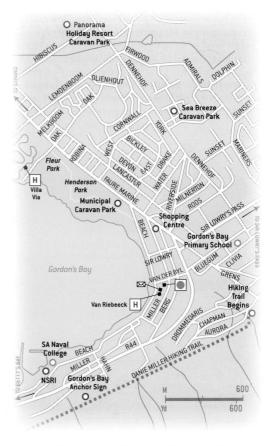

Blushing bride (fynbos).

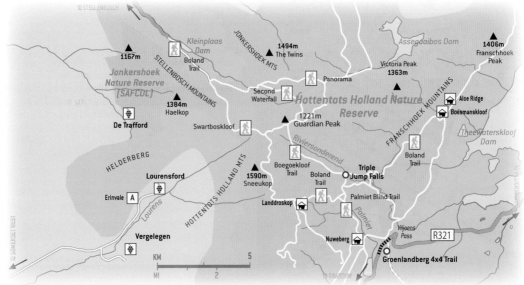

Malmesbury

It's perhaps a combination of the cold upwelling of the Benguela Current (nourishing the dark kelp forests that sway lazily in the wind-blown, big-waved seas) and the stark and rocky coastal landscapes that give the West Coast its wild air. This, coupled with the barren, almost desert-like conditions inland where rain is scarce and summers are ferocious, creates a sometimes-forbidding picture. But that's not taking into account two major rivers: the Orange in the far north (on Namibia's border) and the Olifants, snaking from its mouth to the north of Lambert's Bay into Clanwilliam Dam and through Citrusdal. Both rivers have been harnessed extensively to irrigate citrus orchards, wheatfields and vineyards. As a bonus, at Clanwilliam the Olifants is backed by the craggy, contorted Cederberg mountains. The N7 highway forges a route straight up the West Coast, from Milnerton right up to the Namibian border: crossing the Swartland, it connects Malmesbury (centre for this region's wheat industry and proud home of the country's largest flour mills) with Citrusdal, Clanwilliam and Vanrhynsdorp's spectacular spring-flower displays.

A scenic view of Malmesbury's Swartland.

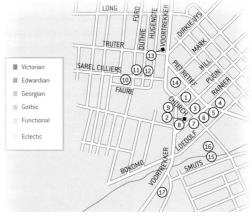

- Victorian
- Edwardian
- Georgian
- Gothic
- Functional
- Eclectic

1 Standard Bank & AM Trust Buildings, 1900
2 Pillars surrounding Town Hall
3 Swartland Dutch Reformed Church, 1860
4 "Oulap" Residence, 1899
5 Trafalgar Centre, mid 19th century
6 Attorneys' Chambers, 1897
7 Land Surveyors' Offices, 1897
8 Old St Thomas Anglican Church,
   now New Apostolic Mission Church, 1859
9 Old Christian Youth Hall,
   now NG Church Office, 1908
10 Baron Von Elgg Stately Home, 1875
11 Town House, 1860
12 19th century streetscape, late 19th century
13 Old Police Station, 1862
14 Twin Shops, 1880
15 Free Mason Lodge, 1866
16 Old Jewish Synagogue,
   now Malmesbury Museum, 1911
17 Andrew's Hope, 1880

MALMESBURY HISTORIC WALK
The local tourist bureau's 'historic route' brochure will guide you through the wide range of architectural styles gracing the town center. There's Gothic Revival style, Georgian, Edwardian, Victorian and even the eclectic twin shops in Piet Retief Street (1880).

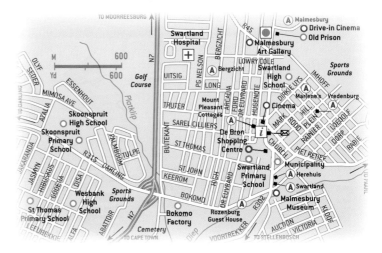

Die Strandloper serves delicious fresh-baked potbrood and seafood in an unpretentious setting: beach sand and reed shelters in a protected cove.

Langebaan

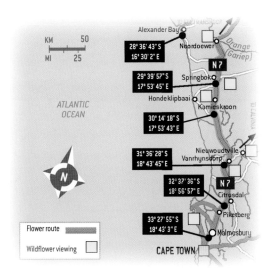

LANGEBAAN

The lagoon is what makes people come back for more to the sleepy town of Langebaan. Part of the West Coast National Park and an important wetland for birdlife, the lagoon's 16km (10-mile) expanse turns a delicate shade of pink at certain times of the year as masses of crimson-winged flamingos descend on its waters. Hartlaub's Gulls, ibis, herons, and curlews also get a look-in, while Cape Cormorants hang out their wings to dry and White Pelicans try hard not to look like clowns. Human action comes in Smartie-pack hues – Hobie cats, windsurfers and para-sailers: name them, they're here.

Pelicans on Langebaan Lagoon.

THE FLOWER ROUTE

Every year between August and October, Spring puts on her prettiest bloom-bedecked frock. The official flower route covers vast distances, from the Tienie Versveld Reserve in Darling to the Orange River in the north, and can take up to three days to cover fully. The arid, stony, scrubby Namaqualand region has different climatic zones, with flower species (4000 at the last count) ranging from neon daisies, gazanias and mesembryanthemums, to hardy fleshy succulents to geophytes (bulbs, corms and tubers) like irises and bulbinellas. Visitors often need travel no further than the Postberg Nature Reserve on Langebaan Lagoon – an hour's drive – to enjoy a mesmerising magic-carpet ride.

> **Top Tip**
> Flowers open with the sun, so cloudy days are no good for viewing. Blooms are best between 11:00 and 16:00; ensure that you drive facing the opened petals, and with the sun behind you.

Flowers in full bloom down the West Coast.

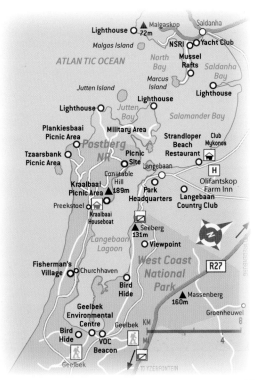

49

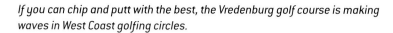
If you can chip and putt with the best, the Vredenburg golf course is making waves in West Coast golfing circles.

Vredenburg, Jacobsbaai, Paternoster & St Helena

VREDENBURG & JACOBSBAAI

All roads lead to Vredenburg ... well, along the coast north of Saldanha, anyway. From here, the west-coast play-zones are all accessible: Jacobsbaai (Jacob's Bay, to those who can't get their tongue around the 'translation'), Paternoster, St Helena and Velddrif. Jacobsbaai is a beautiful, isolated spot of rocky peninsulas and sandy bays, focusing – naturally – on matters of the sea: scuba diving (in crayfish season), angling for linefish, collecting black mussels off the rocks, and dolphin and whale watching (between July and December). If this is waaaay too civilised for you, then rather hit the 17km (10,5-mile) easy-walking hiking trail from Swartriet, just north of Jacobsbaai, to Tietiesbaai. It crosses dune veld, fynbos and rocky coastal terrain; there are no trail facilities and a permit is required from the West Coast Council.

PATERNOSTER & ST HELENA

For a peek at how the fisherfolk live, Paternoster's village of traditional low-slung, small windowed, thatched fishermen's cottages will give you an idea. How did this village get its name? The story goes that when 17th-century Portuguese sailors were shipwrecked here, they recited the Paternoster (Lord's Prayer) to give thanks for their survival. Around the promontory to the north, St Helena Bay is another fishing village perched at the edge of a pretty bay. Some secret recipe of stark rocky coastline and frigid west-coast temperatures appears to have concocted a particularly turquoise hue in the waters of this coast. The coldness also nurtures healthy crayfish (Cape lobster), and scuba divers descend upon both villages in crayfishing season.

Local men and children on their boat.

Locals from Paternoster in front of their home.

> **Top Tip**
> Trails in the Rocher Pan Nature Reserve will expand your nature-bent horizons to activities like fabulous birdwatching, spring flower-gazing, and southern right whale-spying.

Velddrif & Dwarskersbos

VELDDRIF

Velddrif has the advantage of two worlds: cold blue-green seas and the Berg River mouth. Line-fishing, cray-fishing, mussel-catching and sea-based watersports on the one hand, with birdwatching, canoeing, row-boating on the Berg on the other. Velddrif's world has also been enlivened by the development of an upscale holiday resort along its shores, attracting hordes of holidaymakers, come to let their hair down and play.

DWARSKERSBOS

A popular holiday resort, Dwarskersbos lies a quick drive north of Laaiplek and in the middle of the St Helena Bay basin. It boasts a brilliant, sandy beach that stretches as far as the eye can see. Back in '69 the town was wracked by a tidal wave that tore through the dune and swamped a number of houses. Whales can be spotted offshore, and the area has grown in popularity amongst anglers and watersports enthusiasts.

Above: Close-up of fishing boat.
Below: Wooden jetty on Berg River at Velddrif.

Top Tip
Enjoy bird-watching at Rocher Pan Nature Reserve, water sports at Port Owen Marina, local art at the West Coast Art Gallery, and the taste of the local West Coast delicacy, 'bokkom' (a salt fish).

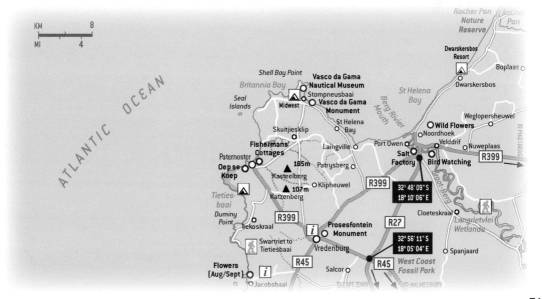

Clanwilliam & Cederberg

The Maltese Cross has been crumbling for centuries – its upper section is made up of stronger Table Mountain sandstone.

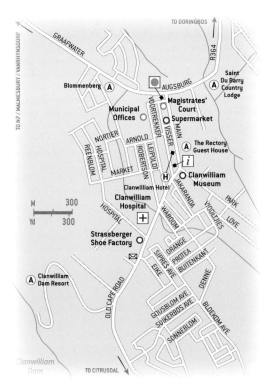

CLANWILLIAM

Another spot on the map whose body of water is more famous than the town: the 18km (11-mile) stretch of lake at the foot of the gnarled, weather-eroded Cederberg mountain range is mini-heaven for boaters and water-skiers. In summer they emerge soon after sunrise from holiday cabins, or the idyllically placed campsite nudging the water's edge, to glide across the dam's mirror-smooth surfaces before the winds stir. The dam, fed by the Olifants River, irrigates the surrounding farmlands and water can often be seen bursting through its sluice gates. The Cederberg mountains and surrounding area are named after the Clanwilliam cedar, which is today a protected species in the Cederberg Wilderness Area.

CEDERBERG HIKING

The Cederberg range is part of the Cape Folded Mountains, its ingredients being sandstone, shale and quartzite, each being open to erosion to varying degrees. The result – powerful biting winds, dissolving rain and abrasion have nimbly and artfully sculpted a moonscape peopled by rocky gargoyles and goblins. No wonder walkers and overnight backpackers can't keep away from this place of bizarre and otherworldly 'creatures'. The 20m-high (65ft) Maltese Cross is a day-hike from Dwarsrivier, the impressive stone Wolfberg Arch (30m / 98ft) is less than a half-day away, and the Wolfberg Cracks are closer still, although it takes some squeezing, slithering and pushing from the rear to get there. Not for the half-hearted! Views from all the sites are quite stupendous. The monoliths of Tafelberg and Sneeuberg (2028m / 6654ft) can also be climbed.

Top Tip
Don't miss out on the San paintings (permits required) in their natural setting of surreal landscapes with names like Amphitheatre and Stadsaal ('city hall') caves; the spirit of such places is awesome.

Over countless centuries wind and water carved the Cederberg into a fairytale landscape: pinnacles, arches and bold fissures now decorate the landscape.

Cederberg

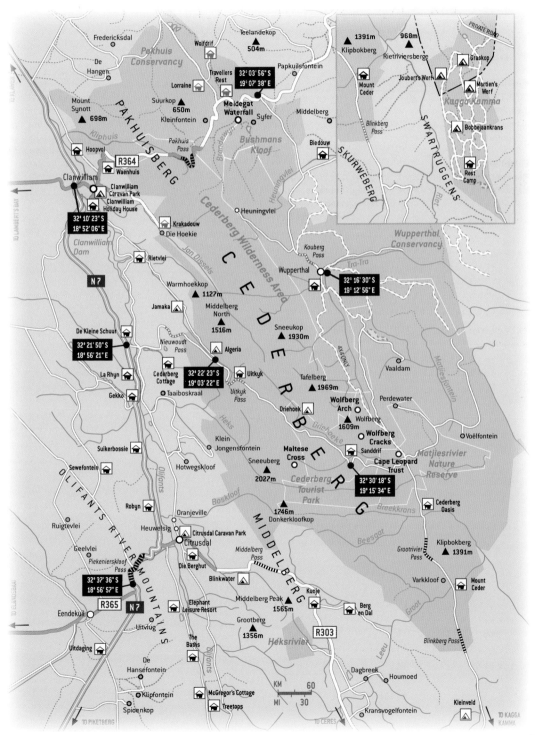

Fredericksdal
Teelandekop
504m
Wolfdrif
Pakhuis Conservancy
De Hangen
Travellers Rest
Papkuilsfontein
32° 03' 56" S
19° 07' 38" E
Lorraine
Meidegat Waterfall
Syfer
Middelberg
Suurkop
650m
Kleinfontein
Mount Synott
698m
Pakhuis Pass
Biedouw
Hoopvol
Heuningvlei
Bushmans Kloof
R364
Waenhuis
Clanwilliam
Clanwilliam Caravan Park
Clanwilliam Holiday House
32° 10' 23" S
18° 52' 06" E
Krakadouw
Die Hoekie
Clanwilliam Dam
Rietvlei
Kouberg Pass
Wupperthal
32° 16' 30" S
19° 12' 56" E
N7
Warmhoekkop
1127m
Jamaka
Middelberg North
1516m
Sneeukop
1930m
De Kleine Schuur
32° 21' 50" S
18° 56' 21" E
Nieuwoudt Pass
Algeria
32° 22' 23" S
19° 03' 22" E
Uitkyk
Tafelberg
1969m
Vaaldam
La Rhyn
Cederberg Cottage
Taaiboskraal
Uitkyk Pass
Driehoek
Wolfberg Arch
Perdewater
Gekko
Wolfberg 1609m
Wolfberg Cracks
Voëlfontein
Suikerbossie
Klein Jongensfontein
Sanddrif
Sewefontein
Hotwegskloof
Sneeuberg
Maltese Cross
Cape Leopard Trust
32° 30' 18" S
19° 15' 34" E
Matjiesrivier Nature Reserve
2027m
Cederberg Tourist Park
Cederberg Oasis
Robyn
Oranjeville
1746m
Donkerkloofkop
Breekkrans
Ruigtevlei
Heuwelsig
Citrusdal Caravan Park
Citrusdal
Beesgat
Klipbokkop
1391m
Geelvlei
Piekenierskloof Pass
Die Berghut
Middelberg Pass
MIDDELBERG
Grootrivier Pass
Varkkloof
Mount Ceder
32° 37' 36" S
18° 56' 57" E
Blinkwater
Kunje
R365 N7
Eendekuil
Elephant Leisure Resort
Middelberg Peak
1565m
Berg en Dal
Uitvlug
Grootberg
1356m
R303
Blinkberg Pass
Vitdaging
The Baths
Heksrivier
De Hanséfontein
Dagbreek
Houmoed
Klipfontein
McGregor's Cottage
KM 60
MI 30
Kleinveld
Spioenkop
Treetops
Kransvogelfontein

PAKHUISBERG

CEDERBERG WILDERNESS AREA

CEDERBERG

OLIFANTS RIVER MOUNTAINS

SWARTRUGGENS

SKURWEBERG

1391m
Klipbokkberg
968m
Rietrivviersberge
Graskop
Mount Ceder
Joubert's Werf
Martien's Werf
Kagga Kamma
Blinkberg Pass
Bobbejaankrans
PRIVATE ROAD
Rest Camp

Wupperthal Conservancy

TO KLAWER
TO LAMBERT'S BAY
TO CITRUSDAL
TO PIKETBERG
TO CERES
TO KAGGA KAMMA

Lambert's Bay & Eland's Bay

LAMBERT'S BAY

Two hours north of St Helena, Bird Island is what makes Lambert's Bay somewhat different. Accessed via a breakwater-cum-harbour wall, you'll smell the guano before you get to see the birds on their island breeding ground. Massed in their thousands are African (Jackass) Penguins, cormorants and Cape Gannets – fairest of them all with their airbrushed faces (could teach us women a thing or too about makeup ...). You can watch the birds' behaviour incognito from a viewing tower.

ELAND'S BAY

This coastline is an extension of the rocky, turquoise-dyed, crayfish-creviced West Coast. Eland's Bay, for one, is – you guessed it – mobbed by divers and their extended families in crayfish season, when the long arm of the law is lifted from December to April. Permits are your ticket to that tender, succulent, sweet-meat (brush with garlic and lemon butter, mmmm ...). A permit from any post office allows daily catches of four per person. On dry land, the terrain makes great offroad territory, and tourist information will supply you with a map of the best 4x4 trails.

Scenic view of gannets on Bird Island.

> **Top Tip**
>
> The Sandveld Museum in Lambert's Bay boasts unusual items, such as an old horse mill, a ginger jar (dated 1652, when Van Riebeeck landed), and a 300-year-old Bible written in High Dutch.

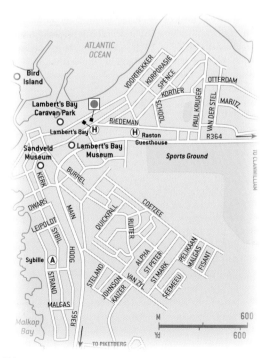

Vanrhynsdorp & Vredendal

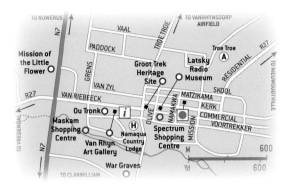

VANRHYNSDORP ▲

This town lies to the west of the Bokkeveld mountain range and is itself at the foot of the Matzikama mountains, settled in the pebble-strewn terrain of the knersvlakte – translating literally as 'gnashing plains'. Can't imagine it's too pleasant in baking mid-summer. Part of the Namaqualand flower route, Vanrhynsdorp's flower displays are mainly succulent vygies and Ursinia daisies. In the town itself, at the end of Voortrekker Street, visitors will find the country's biggest succulent garden and nursery, interesting for its rather outlandish plant forms, while further out is the Matzikama Eco Park. Southeast of Vanrhynsdorp is the Gifberg Pass, gif meaning 'poison' and referring to a poison-leafed bush that's scattered over the slopes. The pass also hides some great examples of San rock art. Views from here take in neatly clipped rows of vines, fields of wheat and rooibos tea of the Olifants River valley.

Handprints on cave wall at Gifberg.

> **Top Tip**
> *Vanrhynsdorp claims to offer the world's only succulent hiking trail, as well as some engrossing waterfalls. Star-gazing at night is also hugely rewarding away from big-city lights!*

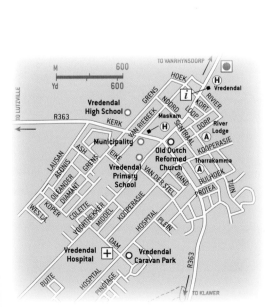

VREDENDAL ◄

Settled along the Lower Olifants River – and the centre of the Olifants irrigation scheme – Vredendal is a major agricultural hub. The town also links travellers with the beaches of the West Coast holiday resorts and is the gateway to Namaqualand and its Pandora's box of blooms. If you arrive at drinking time and you're ready to sip a little wine, Spruitdrift and Vredendal cellars will open their wine-tasting doors. Just hold your breath ... it's still a fledgling wine industry here in the hot, dry Olifants River Valley.

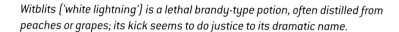

Witblits ('white lightning') is a lethal brandy-type potion, often distilled from peaches or grapes; its kick seems to do justice to its dramatic name.

Worcester

South Africa's forebears definitely weren't kidding when they gave the Overberg its name. The entire region is one of soaring rock walls and chiselled passes – unless you've eased your way to the coastline. And don't be fooled here, either. Wild stormy seas and a deceptively rocky shoreline have seen the demise of a myriad of ships, furnishing Bredasdorp's quirky Shipwreck Museum with quite a collection of artefacts. But there is a gentler side to these seas – dolphins and whales. The most-spotted of the numerous dolphin species are the bottlenose, common and Heaviside's. Even more commonly spotted in-season (July to November) is the southern right whale. Of the world population (between 4000 and 6000) living in the icy sub-Antarctic seas, a great number of these southern rights migrate northward annually. Their gestation period lasts 12 months, they leave their breeding grounds from around June to calve and mate in the warmer, more protected South African coves and bays, often covering distances of up to 2600km (1615 miles) each year.

WORCESTER

Worcester is the biggest centre in the Breede River valley, owing to its industries of fruit, table grapes and winemaking, but the town's appeal lies elsewhere. You can make a splash on the Breede with countless watersport and outdoor activities to choose from, or get stuck into 4x4 trails in the Hex River's mountain territory. Or take it easy and sidle up to some succulents – the largest collection in Africa can be found at the Karoo National Botanic Garden. Ranked by the International Succulent Organisation as among the most authentic in the world, you can measure up to a half-mens tree ('half-human' – go check it out and you'll see why), size up the quiver trees (the San used its hollow bark branches as quivers for their arrows) or stare at the truly prehistoric welwitschias (which can live for thousands of years).

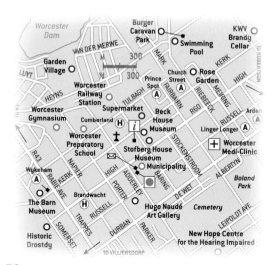

The wreck of the Oriental Pioneer (at a spot locals call Die Skip – the ship) is one of many to succumb along the coast near Agulhas, aka the "Graveyard of Ships".

The Hex River Valley near Worcester.

Robertson & Kleinplasie

ROBERTSON ▶

While Worcester hasn't quite made it in the wine stakes, Robertson comes out with flying colours. Its hot, sunny slopes tempered with plentiful irrigation have produced some powerful, flavour-packed white wines that flaunt themselves with a punch on the nose. Many of Robertson's cellars are award-winners, and you simply can't go wrong by visiting any of these: Bon Courage, De Wetshof, Springfield, Zandvliet or Graham Beck – the latter has an unusual, ultramodern, landscape-blending cellar called Madeba. Not Madiba, our much-loved proponent of peace. Beck's cellar means 'place of running water'.

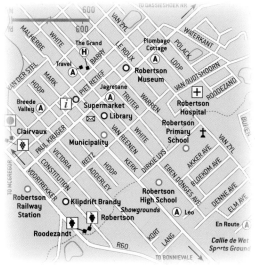

A taproom and restaurant will nourish hungry visitors and slake the deep thirst that sightseeing brings on.

Wine-tasting room, Graham Beck cellar.

KLEINPLASIE ▶

If you're keen to know how people managed before the days of mechanisation, electrification and technology, make a turn at the Kleinplasie Living Open Air Museum. A re-creation of the life lived by Dutch pioneers between 1690 and 1900, there are replicas of a labourer's cottage, a shepherd's hut and a coach house; activities practised daily are represented by a butchery, smithy, dairy and water mill. Year-round activities demonstrate, among others, tobacco-twisting, candlemaking, raisin-making and witblits-distilling. Water is drawn from a well using donkey-power and flour is ground by a horse-drawn mill. Naturally, an adjacent country market sells jams, homemade preserves, honey and cheeses.

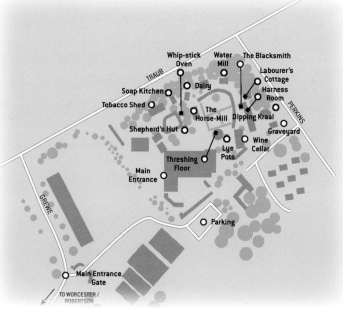

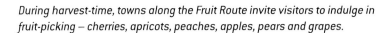

During harvest-time, towns along the Fruit Route invite visitors to indulge in fruit-picking – cherries, apricots, peaches, apples, pears and grapes.

Ceres & Tulbagh

Woman carrying renosterveld near Ceres.

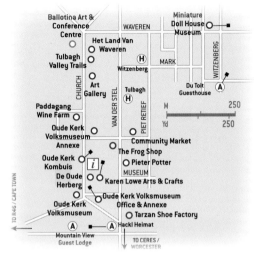

CERES ▼

Ceres nestles in a mountain-fringed basin simply bristling with fruit orchards. Name it and it's likely to feature – apple, pear, peach, nectarine, cherry, orange (even potatoes!). No surprise, then, that the town is named after the Greek goddess of agriculture (or the Roman corn goddess – depending on which way you look at it!). The local fruit-packing plant is the largest in the Southern Hemisphere; if you're serious about your vitamin C, you can embark on a two-hour fruit route. In winter, skiers head for the towering snow-clad Hex River mountains. Michell's Pass to the southwest of Ceres offers jaw-dropping scenery in its precipitous sandstone cliffs and ravines.

TULBAGH ▲

Tulbagh is akin to a living museum, despite its well-recorded earthquake in 1969 – something rather rare in South Africa – which measured 6.3 on the Richter scale and killed 8 people. Beautiful historic houses vie for attention on both sides of Church Street – 32 of the 18th- and 19th-century Cape Dutch and Victorian homes lining its entire length have been declared national monuments. It took five years to meticulously restore the extensive damage caused, and today many house tearooms / restaurants, art galleries, guesthouses and museums cater for tourists. The (very tall) Witzenberg and Winterhoek mountains encircling Tulbagh are heavily sugar-frosted most winters, which also draws the crowds in this generally no-snow country.

Montagu & Swellendam

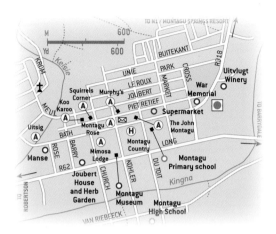

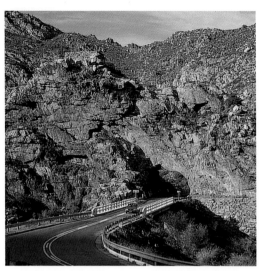

Montagu Pass: high rockfaces and a compelling geological history.

MONTAGU ▲

Yet again, history has left its legacy of historical architecture in this small town. Montagu's charm lies in its homes dating back to the 1850s, with 14 national monuments in Long Street alone. But the town is certainly better known for its natural thermal springs bubbling up at a constant 43 °C from deep within the earth. A hotel and resort has risen around the hot springs and does a humming trade. If the sulphur gets you hot under the collar, an entire series of trails along the northern edge of the Langeberg mountains for hikers, mountain bikers and 4x4 nutters, will get you excited.

SWELLENDAM ▼

At the foot of the Langeberg, gracious old Swellendam has the prettiest spot in the Overberg. The town grew around the Drostdy (magisterial centre), finished in 1746, and now crammed to the hilt with historic edifices – from the Oefeningshuis in Voortrekker Street to the Drostdy (including the Old Jail) and Mayville museums on Swellengrebel. The Oefeningshuis was built as a church to give religious instruction – godsdiensoefening (read: 'educate') – to freed slaves. Note the plaster clockface on the gable with the real clock below it: the story goes, when the real hands matched the plaster clock, it was time for everyone to assemble.

Top Tip
The Old Jail, part of the Drostdy Museum, has a wing of cells, plus a windowless 'black hole'. A trades yard behind the jail features a coppersmith, leather worker, wagon-builder and wheelwright.

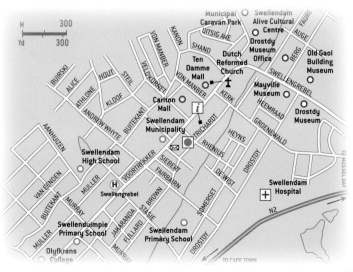

The rooms at the Post House are named after characters from books written by the classic children's author, Beatrix Potter.

Greyton & McGregor

GREYTON ▼
Encroached on by the tall Riviersonderend mountains, Greyton has been sought out by artists, craftspeople and small farmers, who live here in charming little dolls' houses with pitched tin roofs, painted shutters and iron lacework. Don't expect any va-va-voom here – only rest, peace and tranquility. Two guest houses – Greyton Lodge and The Post House, in similar Cape vernacular style – offer delectable dinners and great lodgings if you'd prefer not to have to roll home. A fynbos nature reserve bordering the town has several walking trails that snake into the Riviersonderend mountains.

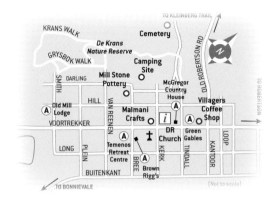

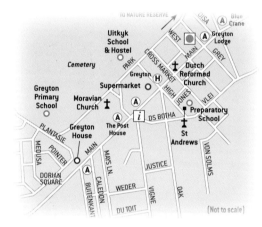

MCGREGOR
Yet another of the country's perfectly preserved (like those old-fashioned pickles) Victorian villages. In an effort not to sound like a scratched gramophone record, the houses here, despite their Victorian influence, have kept to simple Cape lines – whitewashed walls, little square windows, thatched roofs – and without the frills and furbelows.

GREYTON TO MCGREGOR HIKE (BOESMANSKLOOF TRAVERSE) ▼
This 5-hour walking trail through a cleft in the Riviersonderend mountains can be tackled from either village: it's 14km (8,7 miles) from Die Galg, southwest of McGregor, or Main Street, Greyton. The views are great and you get to swim in the pools of the Oakes falls, 9km (5,6 miles) from Greyton. There are no huts; permits are necessary.

Old bicycle outside 'die smouswinkel'.

Since 1552, more than 150 ships have foundered on the southern Cape coast — thats one shipwreck for every kilometre of coastline!

Caledon & Bredasdorp

Museum. The rocky reefs and gale-force winds of this southern stretch of coast (earning the name 'grave-yard of ships') have seen enough shipwrecks to make sure the museum is well-stocked with mini-treasures, artefacts — for example, a medicine chest from the Clan McGregor (1902) — and even blistered ship's figure-heads. The museum, itself housed in the old rectory and church hall, is furnished as a 19th-century townhouse (with a marine flavour, of course).

The Shipwreck museum in Bredasdorp.

> **Top Tip**
> Bredasdorp is the perfect base for exploring a number of nearby nature reserves: De Hoop, De Mond and Heuningberg Nature Reserve, the latter the home of the beautiful and endemic red Bredasdorp lily.

CALEDON ▲

In the late Victorian era in the Overberg, Caledon was once the Southern Hemisphere's most la-di-dah spa. Today, the entertainment era has twirled its baton and transformed the hot mineral springs into a casino, hotel and spa complex. De Overberger Hotel has risen on the site of the old Victorian baths and is now the focus of the fit-'n-healthy, who stay that way with horse riding, tennis and golf. If you're a party-pooper, the Caledon Nature Reserve and Wildflower Garden might show you its 135 protea species. It has bridges and picnic spots, and a 10km (6-mile) trail takes you past the 'window' rock formation (no guessing how it got its name).

BREDASDORP ▶

Surrounded by barley fields and grazing sheep, Bred-asdorp — other than its role as the centre of the wool industry — is the access route to Cape Agulhas and Arniston. Its one and only highlight is its Shipwreck

Haystacks, Caledon surrounds.

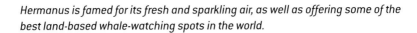
Hermanus

to the mid-1800s. Its Harbour Museum contains fishing artefacts and bleached whalebones. From June to December (peaking during September and October) southern right whales come to calve in Walker Bay, drawing scores of tourists. Walker Bay also nurtures some very fine vines back on dry land and its wineries are creating a real stir.

Hermanus has risen to the ranks of upscale weekend and holiday resort so fast that it has overtaken itself. Massive development and the influx of playthings have made their mark. Sun-worshippers head for the beaches, aficionados of air and water hang-glide, para-glide, windsurf or paddleski, and pubs, restaurants and cafes buzz. Grotto Beach is the trendiest, but those who aren't here to 'be seen' go for long walks or horse-ride along Die Plaat, a silky 12km (8-mile) stretch from the lagoon to De Kelders. Hermanus focuses on the Old Harbour, whose restored fishing boats, lying hull-up, date back

Top: Old Harbour at Hermanus.
Above: Southern right whales.

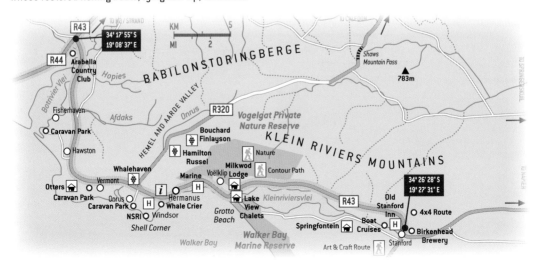

De Hoop Nature Reserve & Breede River

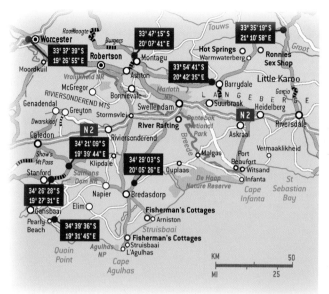

DE HOOP NATURE RESERVE ▼

Two words describe it: simply mag-
nifique! The 50km (31 miles) shoreline
of De Hoop is pristine, particularly the
stretch presided over by 90m-high
(295ft) sand dunes. A marine reserve
extending 5km (3 miles) into the ocean
draws swimmers and divers; a 14km
(9 miles) lagoon pulls wannabe-
ornithologists. A short circular drive to
Tierhoek may reveal the striped Cape
Zebra and small antelopes, while mountain bikers can enjoy various trails in
the Potberg section of the reserve.

BREEDE RIVER VALLEY ▲

The Breede River has an abundance of activities: fruit
routes, a wine route on canoe, river rafting, speed-
boating, boardsailing, even mountain biking and 4x4
trails. Its waters are swelled by tributaries such as the
Hex, Riviersonderend and Kingna. The Breede rises
in the Ceres basin, cutting a deep gorge through the
barrier of mountains that is traversed by the Michell's
Pass. Following the pass road, the river visits Worcester,
Robertson, Bonnievale and Swellendam, emptying into
the Indian Ocean at Witsand.

Stretch of beach in the De Hoop Nature Reserve.

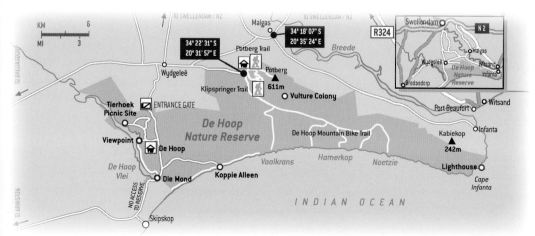

The Wilderness Lakes (a loop of sinuous waterways, lakes, a lagoon and estuary) offer bird-watching trails guaranteed to get you close to the tweeters.

George

When the stretch of coast between Mossel Bay and the Storms River mouth was encountered by early 17th- and 18th-century travellers (who were busy plying the trade routes to the East on their lateen-sailed caravels), the thickly forested slopes had not yet been plundered by rapacious settlers. As a result, their notebooks and diaries were filled with effusive descriptions that – over the centuries – were honed to its present epithet: the Garden Route. French traveller François Le Vaillant recorded his impressions of this coast in 1780 in his diary as 'an enchanted abode'. Today, unfortunately, the remaining stands of indigenous hardwoods – ironwood, yellowwood and stinkwood – are not as pervasive, yet they still manage to make a pretty impressive sight. The entire coastline is fed by countless rivers, drenching rains, and mists sweeping in from the sea, keeping it enduringly moist, fertile and green. This is punctuated by wave-lapped beaches, river mouths, lagoons and lakes, making it the natural playground for outdoor types – walkers and hikers, cyclists and mountain bikers, canoeists and board-sailors.

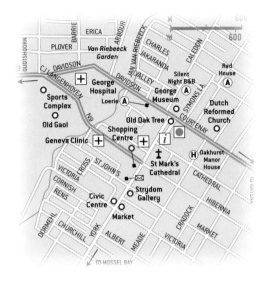

The Fancourt Country Club.

GEORGE
Lying as it does in the shadow of the Outeniqua mountains, it's not surprising that George's heritage smells of newly turned wood. Centre for the timber industry, its indigenous forests of stinkwood and yellowwood have set up more than a few factories. If you're proud of your golf swing, don't miss the luxury Fancourt Hotel and Country Club: gorgeous greens – the 27-hole course is designed by Gary Player – and for non-golfers, gooey kilo-shedding spa treatments to unveil the swan in you.

> **Top Tip**
> The 7-day, 108km (67-mile) Outeniqua hiking trail is popular but tough, over mountains, along a rocky coastline and through heaving forests. Book ahead!

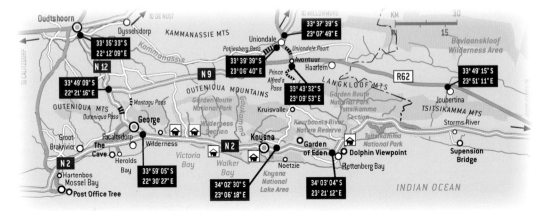

Mossel Bay

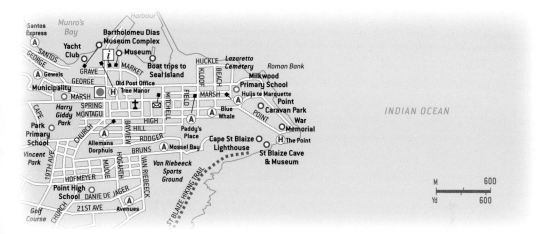

MOSSEL BAY ▲

This spot was first visited in 1488 by Portugese explorer Bartolomeu Dias, who encountered Strandlopers ('beach-wanderers'), a nomadic clan of the Khoi, living off mussels (after which the bay is known) and other yields of the coastline. Mossel Bay is the official start of the Garden Route, but it is more famous for its natural gas deposits, which are converted to oil at the controversial PetroSA development, eking billions out of state coffers. For the idiotically brave, shark cage-dives operate out of the town. Mossel Bay has built a reputation for serving up fantastic mussels, oysters, sole and even marlin.

BARTOLOMEU DIAS MUSEUM COMPLEX ▼

This museum was established in 1988 to celebrate the 500th anniversary of Dias' historic landfall. His 25-ton wooden caravel was reconstructed in Portugal and sailed to Mossel Bay, arriving there in February 1988. The museum was specially modified to accommodate the vessel: an angled roof for the lateen masts and sails, with a sunken floor for its keel. Outside stands a milkwood tree from which a suspended shoe held letters left behind by seafarers. Today, a stone boot acts as a mailbox for visitors' postcards, which are duly marked with a special stamp. Especially pretty are the jewel-bright stained-glass windows commemorating the early voyages of discovery. Even to non-history yobbos, the old maps, photographs and documents detailing early 15th-century explorations are of interest.

Top: Dias museum interior.
Above: Cape St Blaize at the Point, Mossel Bay.

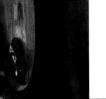

North of Knysna, Noetzie's stone castles (some private homes, some bed-'n'-breakfasts) line a stunning curve of beach, which is accessible via steep stairs.

Knysna

Best done at the Knysna Oyster Co. on Thesen's Island – right next door to Knysna's very own locally brewed, richly flavoured draught ale at Mitchell's Brewery.

KNYSNA LAGOON
The serene 17km-long lagoon is guarded at its sea entrance by two sandstone cliffs, the Knysna Heads. If it's buzz you want, find it at the Knysna Quays Waterfront. Act cool on the terraces of Dry Dock or 34°South, both with great views onto waterways carrying yachts and boats chugging to and fro, where a nearby pedestrian bridge regularly lifts to accommodate passing masts into the marina. When it comes to the locals, Knysna equates to a constituency of Woodstock (leather sandals and tie-dye) and New Age (fairies and crystals).

> **Top Tip**
> From Diepwalle Forest Station in the Kranshoek area, the Elephant Walk Nature Trail threads through towering indigenous trees, also passing the King Edward VII Big Tree (a yellowwood).

A castle at Noetzie.

THE FRESHEST OYSTERS IN TOWN
Every year, in early July, this holiday spot (twice voted the best of the country's tourist towns) puts on her party pearls for the Knysna Oyster Festival. A bountiful supply of the freshest oysters, farmed in the Knysna lagoon, slip their cold slimy way down countless throats, chased by a squeeze of lemon and the fiery breath of Tabasco.

Plettenberg Bay

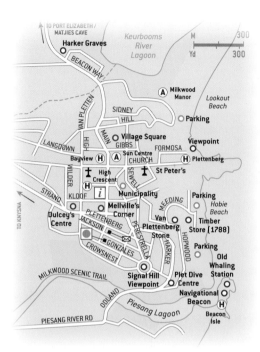

Sea-kayakers on the beach.

PLETTENBERG BAY

If the depth of your pockets rates you in the big bucks league, you'll spend your (local) holidays in this razzle-dazzle town. Perched prettily above a lagoon formed by the Keurbooms and Bitou rivers, 'Plett' (to those who frequent it) in summertime gives you good shopping, better eating, cappuccinos and cocktails, bronzed babes and oiled biceps. When this all gets too much for you, head out to the Robberg Peninsula, a nature and marine reserve where cliff-high walks and tightrope views onto secret-hideaway beaches and the boiling seas below will definitely clear your head. Schools of dolphins riding the waves are not uncommon, likewise whales, in season.

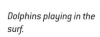

Dolphins playing in the surf.

The camp in the Karoo National Park is highly civilized, with chalets in the Cape vernacular, a pool, restaurant, 4X4 route and even a caravan park.

Beaufort West & Karoo National Park

The Karoo (a vast, dry expanse of desert-like terrain) stretches across sections of the Western Cape and into the Northern Cape. It is divided into the Little and the Great Karoo, according to geological factors as well as topography, vegetation and climate. The name 'karoo' derives from the indigenous Khoi people's description, 'land of great thirst'. Far from devoid of life, the Karoo boasts the world's greatest and largest amount of succulents, with more than 9000 in the Beaufort West region. The scenery is flat, monotonous, and stretches to every horizon, but here and there outcrops bear evidence of typical Karoo shale and sandstone strata, layered like pancakes. At times the monotony of the landscape is also broken by dolerite formations where volcanic lava has thrust up through the earth, and over time been weathered into weird and wonderful shapes as the harder rock resisted the moulding and reshaping forces of wind and water. Some are highly distinctive, with names like the Three Sisters – three similarly shaped conical hills – north of Beaufort West. An enduring image of this slice of South African landscape is, here and there, a lone wind pump, like a sentinel in the crisp, eternally clear Karoo air.

Accommodation in the Karoo National Park.

Still life in Beaufort West.

Top Tip
The Karoo (Hottentot for 'dry thirstland') is a baking, arid and desolate region, and boasts an ancient history that offers up a plethora of fossils from its swamp days.

Beaufort West & Karoo National Park

BEAUFORT WEST

The N1 – the Great North Road, connecting Cape Town with Johannesburg – bisects the Karoo. Beaufort West, the 'capital' of the Karoo region (or at least its largest town!) is located on the N1. The town has little to commend it, other than its role as a centre of civilization in the flat, featureless middle of nowhere. Travellers can find a basic, clean place to stay overnight, fill their travel-weary tums, refuel their equally travel-weary vehicles, and then fill it with lots of treats to stave off boredom from the many hours spent on the road.

KAROO NATIONAL PARK

Just north of Beaufort West, the vast flat plains of the Karoo National Park are deceptive in the sweet green fodder they so obviously provide to kudu, hartebeest and springbok. Other wildlife has been re-introduced, 'big guns' such as black rhino, black wildebeest – 'gnu' is an apt name for a creature that looks like it's stepped out of Jungle Book – and Cape mountain zebra. Animal supreme is the gemsbok, with its rapier horns that seem to rip the air. The park has a 4x4 trail, and the Fossil (geology) and Bossie (vegetation) walking trails.

A grey rhebok family, cleverly camouflaged on a rocky koppie (hill) in the Karoo National Park.

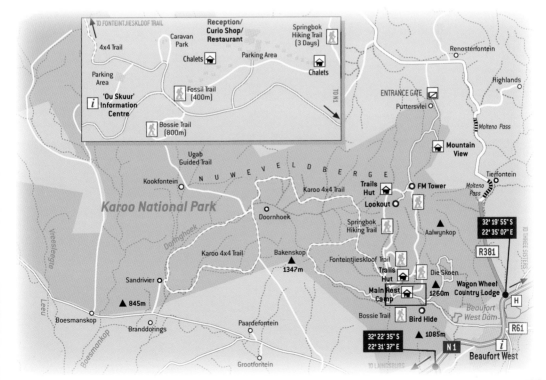

Laingsburg & Matjiesfontein

LAINGSBURG ▼

This town's dubious claim to fame is its brush with momentous floods in 1981. Laingsburg was laid out in 1881, along the banks of the Buffalo River, with a backdrop of rolling hills melding with the Klein Swartberg's sandstone mountain peaks. Ironically, its centenary year (which should have been one of celebration) was marked by uncharacteristically heavy rains, the result of which was that the river burst its banks, flooding the dry, sandy, unstable soils and causing major landslides. Much of the town was covered in river silts and muds. The Dutch Reformed Church was one original old building that remained unscathed.

MATJIESFONTEIN

A turn-of-the-century town centering on the 1900 Lord Milner Hotel, Matjiesfontein is in its entirety a national monument. It was all started by Scotsman James Logan in 1883, when he established a dining place alongside the railway line in an age when trains had no dining coaches. Over time, this expanded to become a hotel and today, Lord Milner's decorative iron-lace verandahs and white-painted square turrets are reminiscent of that elegant time. Despite the lattice-fringed post office nearby, Matjiesfontein is, essentially, a charming hotel complex planted in the middle of the Little Karoo.

The Lord Milner Hotel in Matjiesfontein: its guestbook is a name-droppers' delight!

A secret, stunning world unfolds alongside Seweweekspoort.

> **Top Tip**
> Matjiesfontein boasts some interesting museums (the Transport Museum and the Marie Rawdon Museum), while a trip around town on the local London double-decker bus is a must.

According to local legend, Seweweekspoort ('seven weeks pass') refers to the time it took for early brandy smugglers to cross this mountain barrier.

Oudtshoorn

OUDTSHOORN

The country's ostrich-farming capital has earned its reputation, boasting grandiose sandstone mansions (aka 'feather' palaces), with dyed feathers, ostrich leather handbags, belts, shoes and painted eggs for sale. At the Cango Wildlife Ranch there are lion and cheetah to spy on (from a walkway), and crocodiles and alligators to snap their ugly teeth at you. If you're into 'magic-mushroom trips', visit the Cango Caves for the phantasmagorical limestone drip formations.

FOUR PASSES

Composed of rough-hewn rock and deep sky, the Four Passes has an amazing concentration of mountain landscapes, including the Swartberg, Langeberg and Outeniqua mountains. Pass builder Thomas Bain proved his mettle at the base of these rock barriers. Seweweeks-poort rises to 2325m (7628ft), Schoemanspoort chisels through a 10km (6-mile) narrow chasm, Swartberg winds on for 24km (15 miles) and Meiringspoort bares its cliffs in contorted, burnt-orange folds.

Above: Multi-hued ostrich feathers are on offer.
Left: Ride on an ostrich or cuddle the chicks.

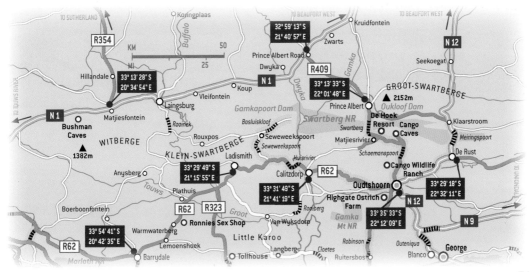

Western Cape Driving Maps

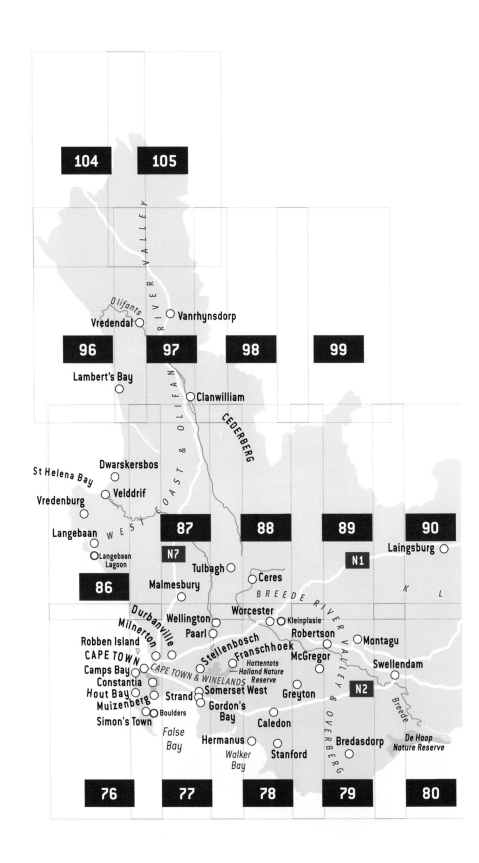

104

105

Olifants

Vredendal ○   ○ Vanrhynsdorp

R I V E R   V A L L E Y

96   97   98   99

Lambert's Bay ○

C O A S T   &   O L I F A N

○ Clanwilliam

CEDERBERG

Dwarskersbos

St Helena Bay   ○

Vredenburg   ○ Velddrif
○

Langebaan ○

W E S T   87   88   89   90

○ Langebaan
Lagoon

N7   Laingsburg ○

86   Tulbagh ○

Malmesbury ○   ○ Ceres   K   L

B R E E D E   R I V E R

Durbanville   Worcester   N1
Milnerton   Wellington ○   ○ Kleinplasie
Paarl ○   Robertson ○   ○ Montagu
Robben Island   Stellenbosch   McGregor ○
CAPE TOWN   Franschhoek ○   Swellendam ○
Camps Bay ○   CAPE TOWN & WINELANDS   Hottentots
Constantia ○   Holland Nature   N2
Hout Bay ○   Strand   Somerset West   Reserve
Muizenberg ○○   Gordon's   ○ Greyton   *Breede*
Simon's Town   Boulders   Bay   Caledon ○
        False   ○ OVERBERG   *De Hoop*
        Bay   Hermanus ○   Bredasdorp   *Nature Reserve*
            Walker   Stanford ○   ○
            Bay

76   77   78   79   80

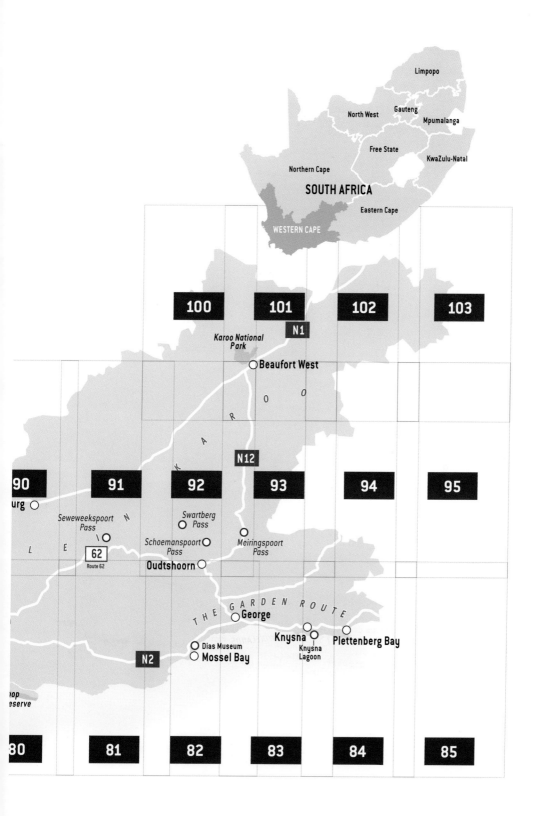

SOUTH AFRICA

Limpopo

North West · Gauteng · Mpumalanga

Free State

Northern Cape · KwaZulu-Natal

Eastern Cape

WESTERN CAPE

| 100 | 101 | 102 | 103 |

N1

Karoo National Park

○ Beaufort West

K A R O O

N12

| 90 | 91 | 92 | 93 | 94 | 95 |

urg ○

Seweweekspoort Pass ○

Swartberg Pass ○

Schoemanspoort Pass ○

Meiringspoort Pass ○

N

L E

62
Route 62

Oudtshoorn ○

THE GARDEN ROUTE

○ George

Knysna ○
Knysna Lagoon

Plettenberg Bay

○ Dias Museum
○ Mossel Bay

N2

op eserve

| 80 | 81 | 82 | 83 | 84 | 85 |

L

M

N

O

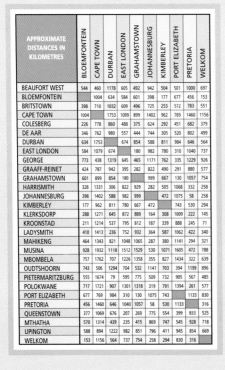

APPROXIMATE DISTANCES IN KILOMETRES	BLOEMFONTEIN	CAPE TOWN	DURBAN	EAST LONDON	GRAHAMSTOWN	JOHANNESBURG	KIMBERLEY	PORT ELIZABETH	PRETORIA	WELKOM
BEAUFORT WEST	544	460	1178	605	492	942	504	501	1000	697
BLOEMFONTEIN		1004	634	584	601	398	177	677	456	153
BRITSTOWN	398	710	1032	609	496	725	253	572	783	551
CAPE TOWN	1004		1753	1099	899	1402	962	769	1460	1156
COLESBERG	226	778	860	488	375	624	292	451	682	379
DE AAR	346	762	980	557	444	744	305	520	802	499
DURBAN	634	1753		674	854	588	811	984	646	564
EAST LONDON	584	1079	674		180	982	780	310	1040	737
GEORGE	773	438	1319	645	465	1171	762	335	1229	926
GRAAFF-REINET	424	787	942	395	282	822	490	291	880	577
GRAHAMSTOWN	601	899	854	180		999	667	130	1057	754
HARRISMITH	328	1331	306	822	929	282	505	1068	332	258
JOHANNESBURG	398	1402	588	982	999		472	1075	58	258
KIMBERLEY	177	962	811	780	667	472		743	530	294
KLERKSDORP	288	1271	645	872	889	164	308	1009	222	145
KROONSTAD	211	1214	537	795	812	187	339	888	245	71
LADYSMITH	410	1413	236	752	932	364	587	1062	422	340
MAHIKENG	464	1343	821	1048	1065	287	380	1141	294	321
MUSINA	928	1932	1118	1512	1529	530	1071	1605	472	788
MBOMBELA	757	1762	707	1226	1358	355	827	1434	322	639
OUDTSHOORN	743	506	1294	704	532	1141	703	394	1199	896
PIETERMARITZBURG	555	1674	79	595	775	509	732	905	567	485
POLOKWANE	717	1721	907	1301	1318	319	791	1394	261	577
PORT ELIZABETH	677	769	984	310	130	1075	743		1133	830
PRETORIA	456	1460	646	1040	1057	58	530	1133		316
QUEENSTOWN	377	1069	676	207	269	775	554	399	833	525
MTHATHA	570	1314	439	235	415	869	747	545	928	718
UPINGTON	588	894	1222	982	851	796	411	945	854	669
WELKOM	153	1156	564	737	754	258	294	830	316	

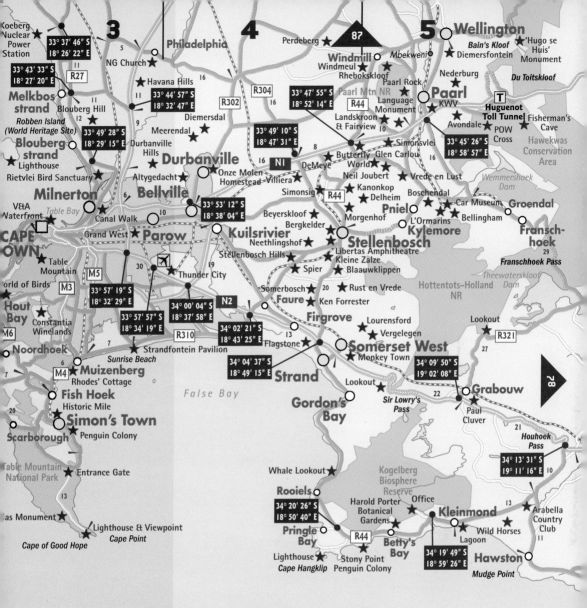

3

Koeberg Nuclear Power Station

33° 37' 46" S 18° 26' 22" E

33° 43' 33" S 18° 27' 20" E

R27

Melkbos strand

Blouberg Hill

Robben Island (World Heritage Site)

Blouberg strand

Lighthouse

Rietvlei Bird Sanctuary

Milnerton

V&A Waterfront

Table Bay

CAPE TOWN

Table Mountain

World of Birds

Hout Bay

Constantia Winelands

Noordhoek

Muizenberg

Rhodes' Cottage

Fish Hoek

Historic Mile

Simon's Town

Penguin Colony

Scarborough

Table Mountain National Park

...as Monument

Cape of Good Hope

Lighthouse & Viewpoint

Cape Point

Philadelphia

NG Church

33° 44' 57" S 18° 32' 47" E

Havana Hills

Diemersdal

Meerendal

Durbanville Hills

Durbanville

Altygedacht

Bellville

33° 53' 12" S 18° 38' 04" E

Grand West

Parow

Kuilsrivier

Neethlingshof

Stellenbosch Hills

Thunder City

33° 57' 19" S 18° 32' 29" E

33° 57' 57" S 18° 34' 19" E

R310

N2

34° 00' 04" S 18° 37' 58" E

34° 02' 21" S 18° 43' 25" E

Flagstone

34° 04' 37" S 18° 49' 15" E

Strand

Sunrise Beach

Strandfontein Pavilion

False Bay

4

Perdeberg

87

Windmill

Windmeul

Rhebokskloof

33° 47' 55" S 18° 52' 14" E

R304

R302

Paarl Mtn NR

Landskroon & Fairview

33° 49' 10" S 18° 47' 31" E

N1

DeMeye

Onze Molen

Homestead

Villiera

Simonsig

Beyerskloof

Bergkelder

Libertas Amphitheatre

Kleine Zalze

Spier

Blaauwklippen

Somerbosch

Faure

Ken Forrester

Firgrove

Lourensford

Vergelegen

Somerset West

Monkey Town

Lookout

Gordon's Bay

Sir Lowry's Pass

Mbekweni

Butterfly World

Neil Joubert

Kanonkop

Delheim

Morgenhof

Stellenbosch

Rust en Vrede

R44

Glen Carlou

Vrede en Lust

Boschendal

Car Museum

Bellingham

L'Ormarins

Pniel

Kylemore

Paul Cluver

Grabouw

R321

Lookout

5

Wellington

Bain's Kloof

Diemersfontein

'Hugo se Huis' Monument

Du Toitskloof

Nederburg

Paarl Rock

Paarl

KWV

Language Monument

Simonsvlei

33° 45' 26" S 18° 58' 57" E

Huguenot Toll Tunnel

Avondale

POW Cross

Fisherman's Cave

Hawekwas Conservation Area

Wemmershoek Dam

Groendal

Franschhoek

Franschhoek Pass

Theewaterskloof Dam

Hottentots-Holland NR

8

34° 09' 50" S 19° 02' 08" E

Houhoek Pass

34° 13' 31" S 19° 11' 16" E

Whale Lookout

Rooiels

34° 20' 26" S 18° 50' 40" E

Pringle Bay

R44

Lighthouse

Cape Hangklip

Harold Porter Botanical Gardens

Office

Stony Point Penguin Colony

Betty's Bay

Kogelberg Biosphere Reserve

Kleinmond

Wild Horses

Lagoon

34° 19' 49" S 18° 59' 26" E

Hawston

Mudge Point

Arabella Country Club

5

★ Bandits
★ Graves   Slanghoek
★ Jason's Hill
Bain's Kloof 'Hugo se Huis'
Monument

△ 88

Merwida

Du Toitskloof 34   ○
Rawsonville ○
N1

33° 42' 16" S
19° 14' 40" E
Du Preez,
Du Toitskloof
& Lorraine

Aufwaerts
& Deetlefs ★

Kirabo,
Daschbosch ★
& Avonroad

T
Huguenot
Toll Tunnel
★ **POW**
Cross   ★ Fisherman's Cave

L

Du Toitskloof

Hawekwas
Conservation
Area

Wemmershoek
Dam

○ Groendal
○ **Franschhoek**

Franschhoek Pass

Hottentots-Holland
NR   29

34° 01' 34" S
19° 12' 41" E ●

R321
Lookout ○
27

M

○ **Grabouw**
★ Paul
Cluver   21

34° 13' 31" S
19° 11' 16" E

△ 77

Houhoek
Pass
Beaumont ★
○ **Botrivier**   9

34° 13' 22" S
19° 16' 49" E

34° 17' 55" S
19° 08' 37" E ●
Arabella Country Club

★ Wild Horses
11   41   **R320**

N

○ **Hawston**
Mudge Point

○ Onrus
★ Hamilton Russell ★ Bouchard Finlayson
Historic Harbour
Hermanus
★ Whale Watching

6

Kleinplasie Open-
Air Museum
★ Drostdy ○ **Worcester**

★ ●

★ Aan-de-Doorns

R400
Mowers ○   48

Greater Brandvlei
Dam

R43
48

○ **Hammanshof**

○ **Bereaville**

★ Theewaterskloof
Country Club

Theewaterskloof
Dam   33

33

R406   Dwarskloof

34° 13' 38" S
19° 25' 44" E

34° 12' 40" S
19° 23' 54" E ●
3   ★ Wildflower
Garden
★ Caledon Casino
& Spa
Caledon ○   39

14

Shaws
Pass

Fernkloof NR   Akkedisberg
River   Pass
Cruises
★ Birkenhead
Brewery
35   23

Stanford ○
34° 26' 28" S
19° 27' 31" E

7

Rooihoogte
Pass

R318

33° 46' 11" S
19° 44' 58" E

Dassieshoe
NR

Cilandia ★   ○ Rooiberg
★ Bon Cap
Graham Beck Reserve ★★
Graham Beck   **R400**
Breë
★ Amathunzi Reserve

Agterkliphoogte ★

Vrolijkhei
Nature Rese

★ Historic Buildings ★
McGregor ○
★ Boesmanskloof Traverse ★
Viljoenshoogte Pass

Riviersonderend
Nature Reserve

Lindeshot ○

34° 10' 07" S
19° 48' 08" E ●

N2
Krige   **R326**

○ Jongensklip
27

○ **Genadendal**
○ **Greyton**
R406

Langkuil

Oukraal ○
34° 21' 09" S
19° 39' 44" E

★ Arch Rock **Fairfield** ○   26
Salmons   **R316**
Dam NR

Feeshuis ★
Art Gallery
and Toy Museu

★ Papiesvlei ○   ★ Moravian Church
& Clock
○ **Elim**
★ Historic Waterm
11
34° 30' 59" S
19° 25' 32" E

Shark
Cage Diving ★
○ **Gansbaai**
Lighthouse ★
Danger Point
★ Birkenhead
Wreck 1852

Walker Bay
Marine Reserve   22

Grootbos
Private NR

Boat trips to ○ **Kleinbaai**
Dyer Island Sandy Point
◇ Dyer Island

41

O

Baardskeerdersbos ○

○ **Pearly Beach**   37
Bantamsklip **R43**
Shell Point

★ Wolvengat Gallery

Soetendals
Vlei

34° 39' 36" S
19° 31' 45" E

Quoin Point

34° 44' 44" S
19° 39' 22" E

○ **Die Dam**

Hoëkra

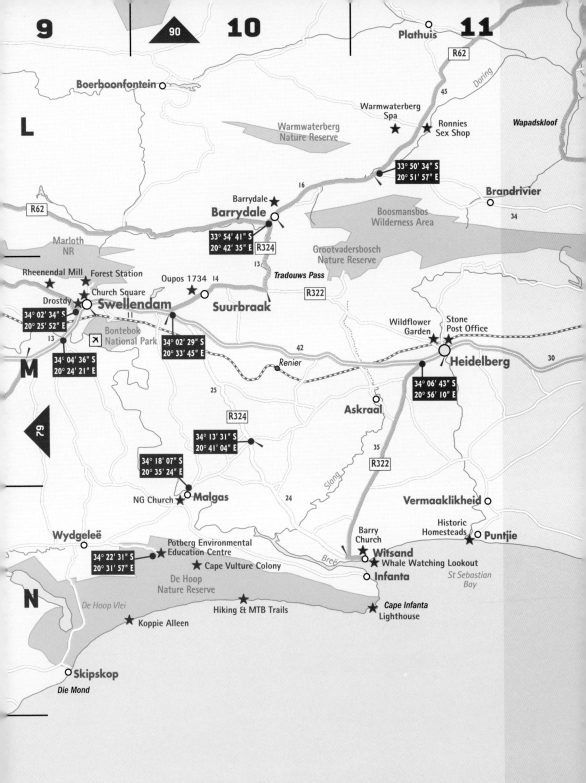

90

79

Plathuis

R62

Doring

Boerboonfontein

L

Warmwaterberg
Nature Reserve

Warmwaterberg
Spa

45

Wapadskloof

Ronnies
Sex Shop

R62

33° 50' 34" S
20° 51' 57" E

Brandrivier

16

Barrydale

34

Barrydale

Boosmansbos
Wilderness Area

Marloth
NR

33° 54' 41" S
20° 42' 35" E

R324

Grootvadersbosch
Nature Reserve

13

Rheenendal Mill

Forest Station

Oupos 1734

14

Tradouws Pass

Church Square

Drostdy

R322

Swellendam

Suurbraak

34° 02' 34" S
20° 25' 52" E

11

Wildflower
Garden

Stone
Post Office

M

Bontebok
National Park

34° 02' 29" S
20° 33' 45" E

42

Heidelberg

30

34° 04' 36" S
20° 24' 21" E

13

Renier

34° 06' 43" S
20° 56' 10" E

25

R324

Askraal

34° 13' 31" S
20° 41' 04" E

35

34° 18' 07" S
20° 35' 24" E

R322

Slang

Vermaaklikheid

NG Church

Malgas

24

Historic
Homesteads

Puntjie

Wydgeleë

Potberg Environmental
Education Centre

Barry
Church

Cape Vulture Colony

Breë

Witsand

34° 22' 31" S
20° 31' 57" E

De Hoop
Nature Reserve

Whale Watching Lookout

N

De Hoop Vlei

Hiking & MTB Trails

Infanta

*St Sebastian
Bay*

Koppie Alleen

Cape Infanta
Lighthouse

Skipskop

Die Mond

O

ROOIBERG

91
Rooiberg Pass

★ Calitzdorp Spa (Hot Springs)

Gamka Mt NR

OUTENIQUABERGE

R327

55

Van Wyksdorp ●

33° 44' 42" S
21° 27' 08" E

Wapadskloof

Groot

Outeniqua NR

40

R323

33° 51' 20" S
21° 26' 26" E

33° 54' 28" S
21° 22' 29" E

34

3

26

Langberg ●

41

Cloetes Pass

33° 55' 04" S
21° 13' 13" E

Boosmansbos
Wilderness Area

★ Toll House

22

Garcia Pass

Die Poort ★

Herbertsdale ●

★ St Barnabas
Anglican Church

Du Plessis
Pass

LANGEBERG

★ Zeekoegat

Africana Centre ★ ● Riversdale

30

✈

34° 05' 36" S
21° 15' 04" E

12

R327

82

Dekriet ●

N2

Gourits ●

34° 10' 13" S
21° 19' 23" E

25

Albertinja ●

21 Gouritz River
Bridge ★

R305

Aloe Vera Factory ★

34° 11' 59" S
21° 40' 36" E

Droëvlakte ●

34° 12' 43" S
21° 36' 01" E

Gourits

Riethuiskraal ●

27

34

Johnson's Post ●

Still Bay East
Geelkrans & Pauline
Bohnen Nature Reserves

Gouritsmond ●

Palinggat Homestead ★

Trinity
Point

Lighthouse

Bird Hide ★ ● Still Bay West
★ Morris Point   Still Bay

Groot
Jongensfontein ●

Ancient Fish Traps (Visvywers)

★ Ystervarkpunt

Cape
Barracouta

92

★ Safari Ostrich Farm
★ Suspension Bridge

Kammanassie Dam

★ Calitzdorp Spa (Hot Springs)

★ Highgate Ostrich Farm

33

N12

Koutjie

Gamka Mt NR

23

Blossoms ○

OUTENIQUABERGE

L

Attaquaskloof Monument ★

Swartberg State Forest

25

33° 49' 09" S
22° 21' 16" E

Eseljagpoort
Montagu Pass & Old Smithy
★

○ **Herold**

Outeniqua NR

Doringrivier Wilderness Area

Witfontein State Forest

26 Old 'Smithy'

Topping
★

Outeniqua NR

Cloetes Pass

Robinson Pass

Jonkersberg State Forest

Outeniqua Pass

★ Old Tollhouse

Blanco ★ Fancourt

Eight Bells ● ★ Ruiterbosch

R328

Red Berry Farm ★

George

○ **Herbertsdale**

29

Botlierskop Game Farm

Groot Brakrivier

Bird Farm ★

✈

Garden Route Mall

6
★

Victoria Bay

★ St Barnabas Anglican Church

N2

34° 00' 40" S
22° 22' 58" E

27

Stone Church
★

Du Plessis Pass

★

23

Glentana ○

Pacaltsdorp

Rooiklip

R327

34

34° 06' 46" S
22° 06' 26" E

The Cave ★

Herolds Bay

Oubaai

M

34° 10' 53" S
22° 02' 47" E

Mossel Bay

Hartenbos

Bartolomeu Dias Museum Complex

Bartelsfontein Petro SA

✈ 9

★ **Mossel Bay** ●

18

5

★ Lighthouse
Cape St Blaize

18

34° 10' 44" S
21° 57' 38" E

6

Dana Bay

Garden Route Casino

★★

Post Office Tree

Gourits

Vlees Bay

Johnson's Post ○

○ Vlees Bay

Cape Vacca (Kanonpunt)

N

○

Gouritsmond

O

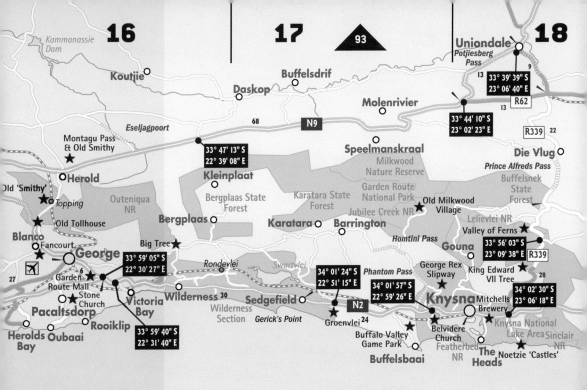

Kammanassie Dam

Koutjie

Buffelsdrif

Daskop

Molenrivier

Uniondale
Potjiesberg Pass

13
33° 39' 39" S
23° 06' 40" E
9
R62

13

33° 44' 10" S
23° 02' 23" E

R339 22

Die Vlug

Prince Alfreds Pass

Eseljagpoort

68

N9

Speelmanskraal

Milkwood Nature Reserve

Buffelsnek State Forest

Montagu Pass & Old Smithy

Herold

Old 'Smithy'

Topping

Old Tollhouse

Blanco
Fancourt

George

Big Tree

33° 59' 05" S
22° 30' 27" E

33° 47' 13" S
22° 39' 08" E

Kleinplaat

Bergplaas State Forest

Karatara State Forest

Garden Route National Park

Old Milkwood Village

Jubilee Creek NR

Bergplaas

Karatara

Barrington

Lelievlei NR

Valley of Ferns

Outeniqua NR

27

Garden Route Mall

Stone Church

Pacaltsdorp

Rooiklip

Herolds Bay
Oubaai

Victoria Bay

Wilderness

30

Rondevlei

Swartvlei

Wilderness Section

Gerick's Point

Sedgefield

Groenvlei

24

34° 01' 24" S
22° 51' 15" E

N2

Phantom Pass

34° 01' 57" S
22° 59' 26" E

Homtini Pass

Gouna

George Rex Slipway

King Edward VII Tree

33° 56' 03" S
23° 09' 38" E

R339

28

Knysna

Mitchells Brewery

34° 02' 30" S
23° 06' 18" E

Knysna National Lake Area

Sinclair NR

33° 59' 40" S
22° 31' 40" E

Buffalo Valley Game Park

Belvidere Church

Featherbed NR

The Heads

Noetzie 'Castles'

Buffelsbaai

INDIAN OCEAN

84

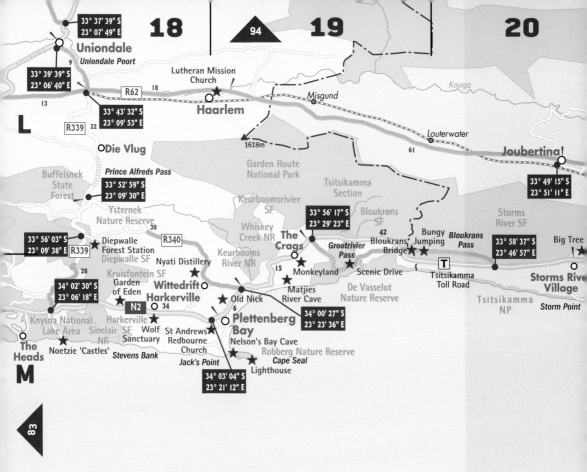

33° 37' 39" S
23° 07' 49" E

Uniondale
Uniondale Poort

9

33° 39' 39" S
23° 06' 40" E

13

R62   18

L

R339   22

Die Vlug

Prince Alfreds Pass

33° 43' 32" S
23° 09' 53" E

*Buffelsnek
State
Forest*

33° 52' 59" S
23° 09' 30" E

*Ysternek
Nature Reserve*

30

*Lutheran Mission
Church*

★ **Haarlem**

1618m

Kouga

Misgund

Louterwater

61

*Garden Route
National Park*

*Tsitsikamma
Section*

Joubertina

33° 49' 15" S
23° 51' 11" E

33° 56' 03" S
23° 09' 38" E

R339

R340

28

*Diepwalle
Forest Station*
Diepwalle SF

Nyati Distillery ★

*Keurboomsrivier
SF*

*Whiskey
Creek NR*

**The
Crags**

33° 56' 17" S
23° 29' 23" E

*Grootrivier
Pass*

★

Bloukrans
Bridge ★ ★

*Storms
River SF*

42   Bungy
Jumping ★ ★

*Bloukrans
Pass*

*Bloukrans
SF*

33° 58' 37" S
23° 46' 57" E

Big Tree
★

Kruisfontein SF

34° 02' 30" S
23° 06' 18" E

*Garden
of Eden*

Wittedrift
Harkerville

N2   34

*Keurbooms
River NR*

15

Monkeyland ★

★ Old Nick

*Matjies
River Cave*

34° 00' 27" S
23° 23' 36" E

Scenic Drive

T

*Tsitsikamma
Toll Road*

*De Vasselot
Nature Reserve*

**Storms River
Village**

*Tsitsikamma
NP*

Storm Point

**The
Heads**

M

*Knysna National
Lake Area*

*Sinclair
NR*

Harkerville ★

★ Noetzie 'Castles'

Wolf
Sanctuary ★

*St Andrews
Redbourne
Church*

**Plettenberg
Bay**

6

Nelson's Bay Cave

Jack's Point

Stevens Bank

Cape Seal

Lighthouse

Robberg Nature Reserve

34° 03' 04" S
23° 21' 12" E

◀ **83**

N

INDIAN OCEAN

O

Cambria

Baviaanskloof
Wilderness Area

Joubertina

33° 49' 15" S
23° 51' 11" E

Heights

Kouga

R62

Kammiebos

33° 56' 56" S
24° 16' 55" E

Storms
River SF

Formosa
Nature Reserve

45

Assegaaibos

33° 58' 06" S
23° 55' 53" E

Storms River Bridge
(Paul Sauer Bridge)

33° 58' 37" S
23° 46' 57" E

Big Tree

Kareedouw

35

15

18

33° 59' 56" S
24° 14' 08" E

Storms River
Village

7

Clarkson

Suspension Bridge
& Hiking Trails

Woodlands

8

21

R102

Tsitsikamma
NP

19

8

Storm Point

Storms River
Mouth

Grootkrans

Voëlkrans

Oubosstrand

20

Oskraal

Houtkapplek

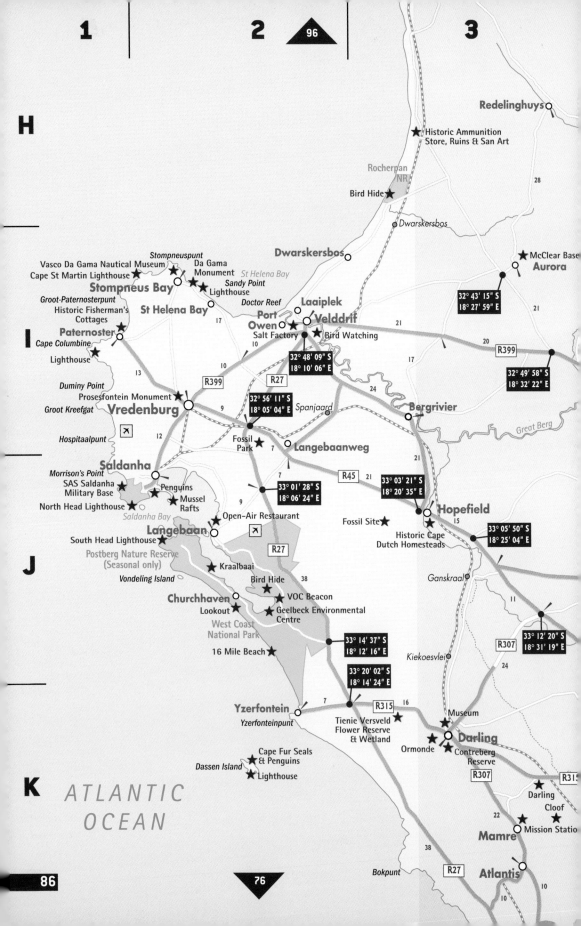

Redelinghuys

★ Historic Ammunition Store, Ruins & San Art

Rocherpan NR

Bird Hide ★

Dwarskersbos

Dwarskersbos

★ McClear Base
○ Aurora

Vasco Da Gama Nautical Museum
Cape St Martin Lighthouse
Stompneuspunt
Da Gama Monument
St Helena Bay
Sandy Point Lighthouse

■ 32° 43' 15" S
18° 27' 59" E

Stompneus Bay
St Helena Bay
Doctor Reef
Laaiplek
Velddrif
Port Owen
Bird Watching
Salt Factory

Groot-Paternosterpunt
Historic Fisherman's Cottages

Paternoster
Cape Columbine

I

Lighthouse

■ 32° 48' 09" S
18° 10' 06" E

21

■ 32° 49' 58" S
18° 32' 22" E

20 R399

Duminy Point
Prosesfontein Monument ★
Groot Kreefgat

Vredenburg

■ 32° 56' 11" S
18° 05' 04" E

R399 R27

Spanjaard

Bergrivier

Great Berg

Hospitaalpunt ✈

Fossil Park ★

Langebaanweg

24

17

21

Saldanha
Morrison's Point
SAS Saldanha Military Base
North Head Lighthouse
Penguins
Mussel Rafts
Saldanha Bay

Open-Air Restaurant

■ 33° 01' 28" S
18° 06' 24" E

R45 21

Fossil Site ★

■ 33° 03' 21" S
18° 20' 35" E

Hopefield

■ 33° 05' 50" S
18° 25' 04" E

Langebaan
South Head Lighthouse
Postberg Nature Reserve (Seasonal only)
Vondeling Island

✈ R27

Kraalbaai
Bird Hide ★
VOC Beacon
Geelbeck Environmental Centre

38

Historic Cape Dutch Homesteads

15

Ganskraal

11

J

Churchhaven
Lookout
West Coast National Park
16 Mile Beach ★

■ 33° 14' 37" S
18° 12' 16" E

Kiekoesvlei

■ 33° 12' 20" S
18° 31' 19" E

R307

24

■ 33° 20' 02" S
18° 14' 24" E

Yzerfontein
Yzerfonteinpunt

7 R315 16

Tienie Versveld Flower Reserve & Wetland ★

Museum ★
★ Darling
Ormonde ★
Contreberg Reserve ★

R307 R315

Cape Fur Seals & Penguins
Dassen Island
★ Lighthouse

Darling Cloof ★

★ ★
○ Mission Statio

22

K ATLANTIC OCEAN

Mamre

Bokpunt

R27 Atlantis

38

10

10

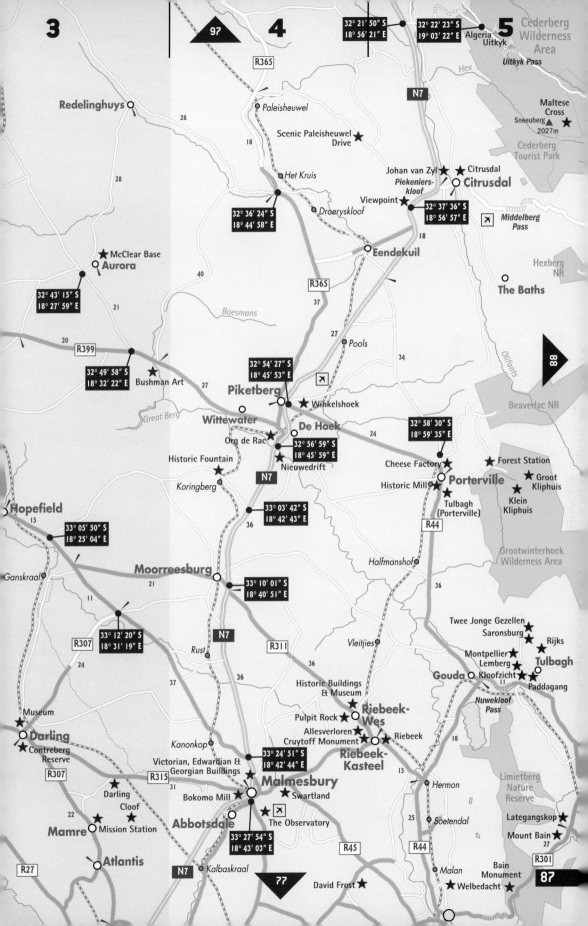

4

32° 21' 50" S
18° 56' 21" E

32° 22' 23" S
19° 03' 22" E

Algeria
Uitkyk

Cederberg
Wilderness
Area

Uitkyk Pass

Hex

N7

Maltese
Cross
Sneeuberg ▲ ★
2027m

Cederberg
Tourist Park

Redelinghuys

Paleisheuwel

26

18

Scenic Paleisheuwel ★
Drive

Het Kruis

Johan van Zyl ★ ★ Citrusdal
*Piekeniers-
kloof*
Viewpoint ★ ● Citrusdal
Droeryskloof

32° 37' 36" S
18° 56' 57" E

✈ *Middelberg
Pass*

Hexberg
NR

The Baths

32° 36' 24" S
18° 44' 58" E

McClear Base ★
Aurora ○

32° 43' 15" S
18° 27' 59" E

40

Eendekuil ●

R365

18

R365

28

21

20

R399

Boesmans

37

27

Pools ●

34

Olifants

88

Beaverlac NR

32° 49' 58" S
18° 32' 22" E

Bushman Art

27

Great Berg

32° 54' 27" S
18° 45' 53" E

✈

Piketberg ●

Wittewater ●

De Hoek ●

★ Winkelshoek

Org de Rac ●

32° 56' 59" S
18° 45' 59" E

Nieuwedrift ●

N7

32° 58' 30" S
18° 59' 35" E

24

Cheese Factory ★ ★ ★ Forest Station
Porterville ●
Historic Mill ★ ● ★ Groot
Kliphuis

Tulbagh
(Porterville) ★

Klein
Kliphuis

Historic Fountain ★

Koringberg

Hopefield ○

15

33° 05' 50" S
18° 25' 04" E

Ganskraal

11

33° 03' 42" S
18° 42' 43" E

36

R44

Halfmanshof ●

Grootwinterhoek
Wilderness
Area

36

Moorreesburg ●

21

33° 10' 01" S
18° 40' 51" E

R307

24

33° 12' 20" S
18° 31' 19" E

N7

Rust

R311

Vleitjies ●

36

Twee Jonge Gezellen ★
Saronsburg ★
Rijks ★
Montpellier ★
Lemberg ★ Tulbagh ●
Gouda ● ● Kloofzicht ★
11 ● Paddagang

37

36

Historic Buildings
& Museum ★
Pulpit Rock ★ Riebeek- ★
Wes ●
Allesverloren ★ ★ Riebeek
Cruytoff Monument ★

*Nuwekloof
Pass*

18

Museum ★
Darling ○ ★
★ Contreberg
Reserve

R307

R315

Kanonkop ●

Victorian, Edwardian &
Georgian Buildings ★
Bokomo Mill ●

31

33° 24' 51" S
18° 42' 44" E

Riebeek-
Kasteel ●

15

Hermon ●

Limietberg
Nature
Reserve

Darling ★
Cloof ★

Malmesbury ●
★ Swartland

25 Soetendal ●

Lategangskop ★

22

Mamre ○ ★ Mission Station

Abbotsdale ○ ● ✈
The Observatory

Mount Bain ★

27

R27

Atlantis ○

N7

Kalbaskraal ●

33° 27' 54" S
18° 43' 03" E

R45

R44

Malan ●

Bain
Monument ●

R301

87

David Frost ★

Welbedacht ●

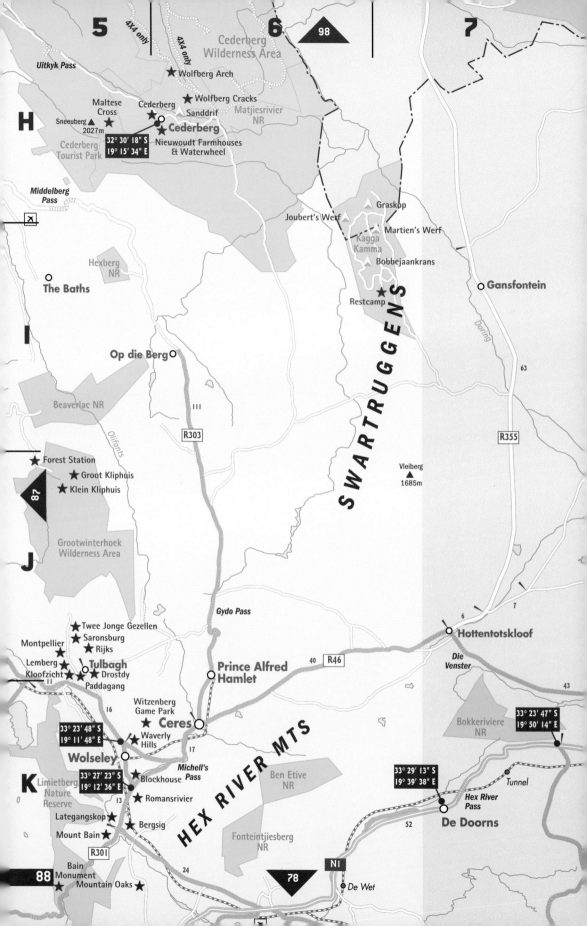

5

4X4 only
4X4 only

Cederberg
Wilderness Area

6 ▲ **98**

7

Uitkyk Pass

★ Wolfberg Arch

Maltese
Cross   Cederberg ○
★   ★   ○   ★ Wolfberg Cracks
Sneeuberg ▲ ★ Sanddrif
2027m   ★ **Cederberg**

Matjiesrivier
NR

H

**32° 30' 18" S
19° 15' 34" E**

★ Nieuwoudt Farmhouses
& Waterwheel

Cederberg
Tourist Park

*Middelberg
Pass*

✈

Graskop
★
Joubert's Werf   ★ Martien's Werf

Kagga
Kamma

Bobbejaankrans

○ **Gansfontein**

The Baths ○

Hexberg
NR

★
Restcamp

I

S W A R T R U G G E N S

Op die Berg ○

Doring

Beaverlac NR

63

Olifants

III

R303

▲ Vleiberg
1685m

R355

★ Forest Station

★ Groot Kliphuis

▲ **87**

★ Klein Kliphuis

J

Grootwinterhoek
Wilderness Area

Gydo Pass

6

7

★ Twee Jonge Gezellen

○ **Hottentotskloof**

★ Saronsburg

*Die
Venster*

Montpellier ★

★ Rijks

Lemberg ★ ★ ★ **Tulbagh**
Kloofzicht ★ ★ ★ Drostdy
Paddagang

**Prince Alfred
Hamlet** ○

40 **R46**

43

**33° 23' 47" S
19° 50' 14" E**

Witzenberg
Game Park

Bokkeriviere
NR

**33° 23' 48" S
19° 11' 48" E** ● ★ **Ceres** ○

16

H E X   R I V E R   M T S

★ Waverly
Hills

Wolseley ○

17

**33° 27' 23" S
19° 12' 36" E** ● ★ Blockhouse

**33° 29' 13" S
19° 39' 38" E**

K

Limietberg
Nature
Reserve

*Michell's
Pass*

Ben Etive
NR

Tunnel

0

13

★ Romansrivier

*Hex River
Pass* ○

★ Lategangskop

★ Bergsig

52

De Doorns

Mount Bain ★

Fonteintjiesberg
NR

R301

24

N1

▼ **78**

▼ **88**

Bain
Monument
★   ★ Mountain Oaks

○ *De Wet*

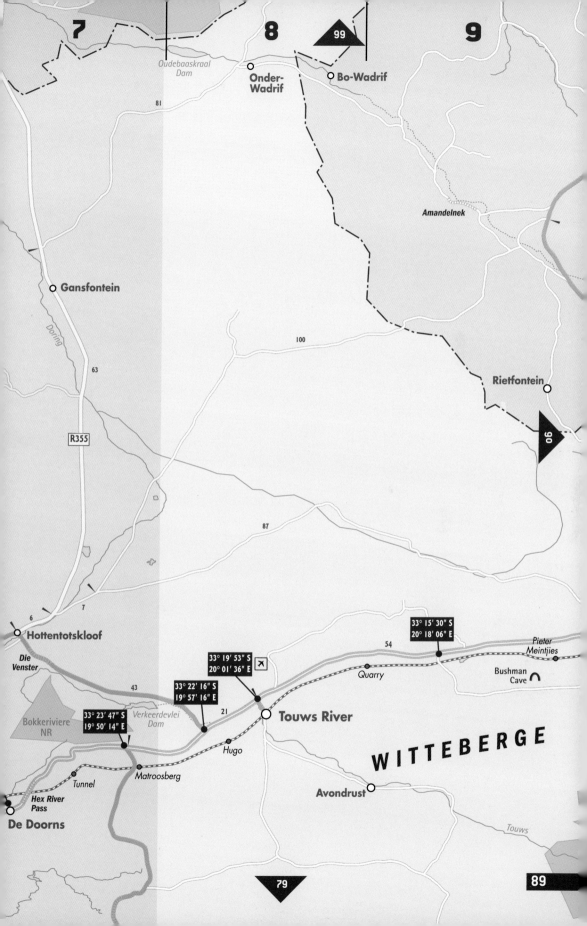

99

Oudebaaskraal
Dam

Onder-
Wadrif

Bo-Wadrif

81

Amandelnek

Gansfontein

Doring

100

63

Rietfontein

R355

90

87

54

Pieter
Meintjies

33° 15′ 30″ S
20° 18′ 06″ E

Bushman
Cave

Hottentotskloof

6

7

Die
Venster

Quarry

33° 19′ 53″ S
20° 01′ 36″ E

43

33° 22′ 16″ S
19° 57′ 16″ E

21

Bokkeriviere
NR

Verkeerdevlei
Dam

33° 23′ 47″ S
19° 50′ 14″ E

Touws River

Hugo

WITTEBERGE

Tunnel

Matroosberg

Avondrust

Hex River
Pass

De Doorns

Touws

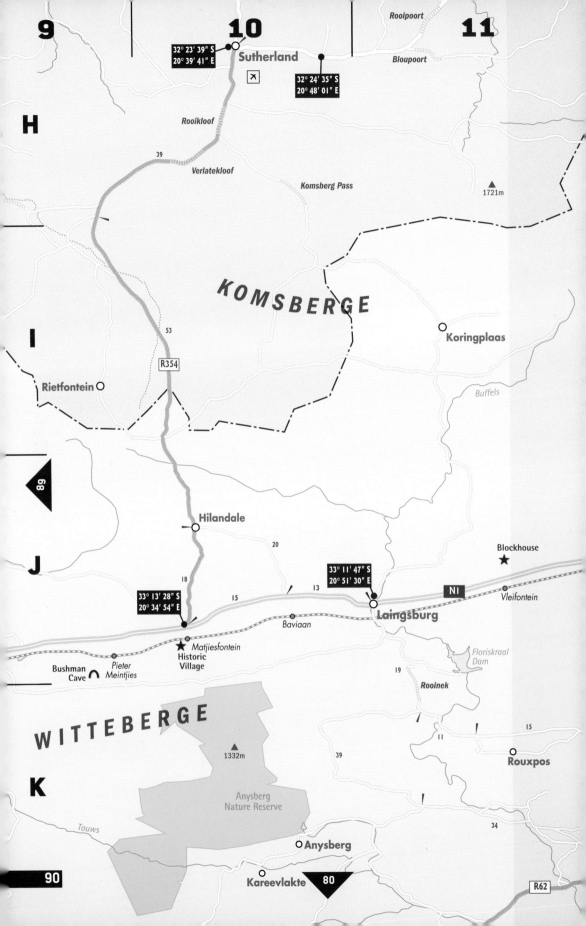

H

32° 23' 39" S
20° 39' 41" E

○ Sutherland

✈

●
32° 24' 35" S
20° 48' 01" E

Rooipoort

Bloupoort

Rooikloof

39

Verlatekloof

Komsberg Pass

▲
1721m

KOMSBERGE

I

53

○ **Koringplaas**

R354

Buffels

Rietfontein ○

◄ 88

Hilandale ○

20

Blockhouse
★

J

18

33° 11' 47" S
20° 51' 30" E

●

N1

Vleifontein ○

15

13

33° 13' 28" S
20° 34' 54" E

●

Baviaan ●

Laingsburg ○

★ *Matjiesfontein*
**Historic
Village**

*Floriskraal
Dam*

Bushman ∩
Cave   *Pieter
Meintjies* ●

19

Rooinek

WITTEBERGE

11

15

▲
1332m

39

○ **Rouxpos**

K

Touws

*Anysberg
Nature Reserve*

34

○ **Anysberg**

Kareevlakte ○   ▼ 80

R62

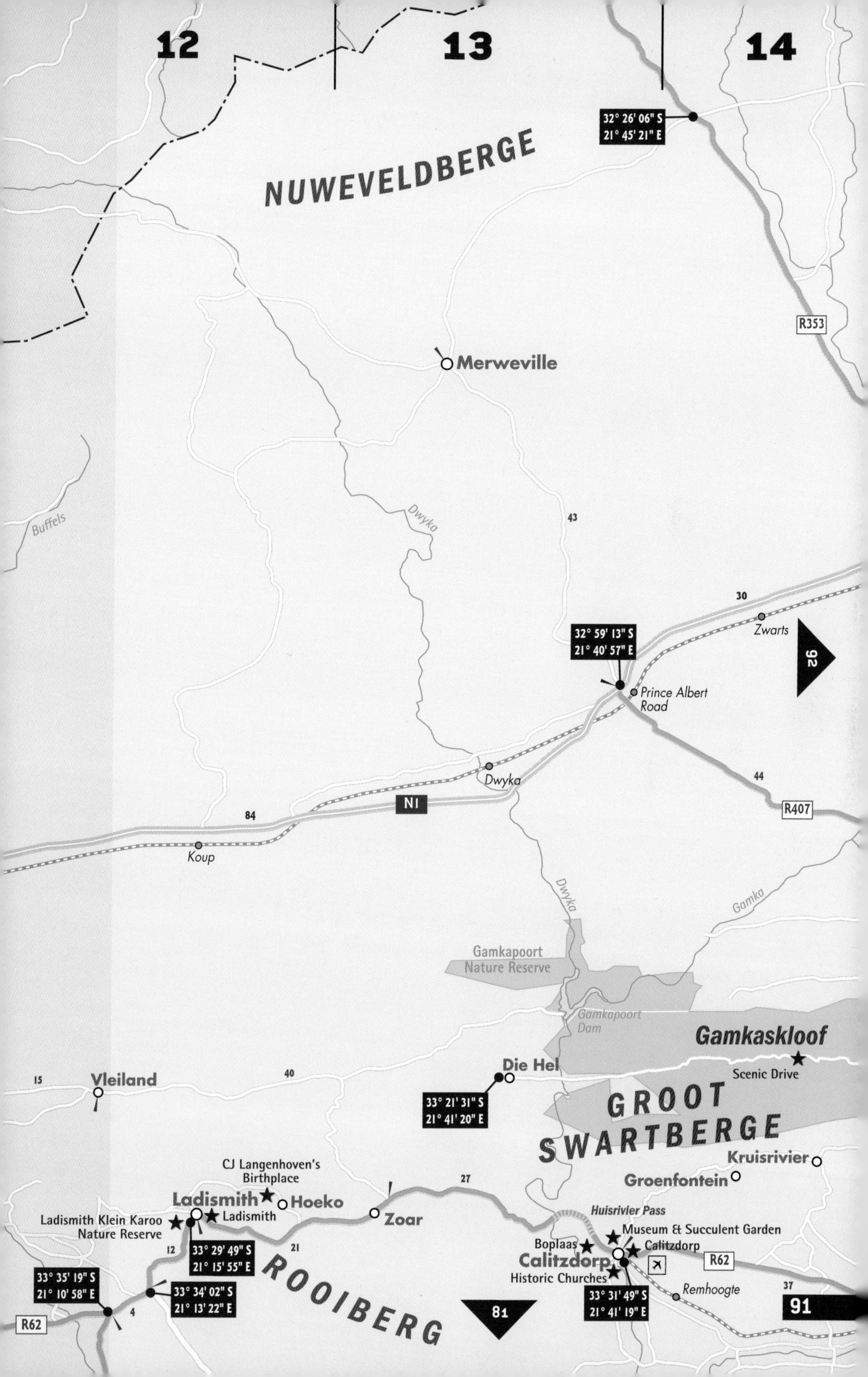

NUWEVELDBERGE

Buffels

Merweville

Dwyka

32° 26' 06" S
21° 45' 21" E

R353

43

30

32° 59' 13" S
21° 40' 57" E

Zwarts

92

Prince Albert
Road

44

Dwyka

R407

84

N1

Koup

Dwyka

Gamka

Gamkapoort
Nature Reserve

Gamkapoort
Dam

Gamkaskloof

Scenic Drive

15

Vleiland

40

Die Hel

33° 21' 31" S
21° 41' 20" E

GROOT
SWARTBERGE

Kruisrivier

CJ Langenhoven's
Birthplace

Groenfontein

27

Huisrivier Pass

Ladismith ★ ○ Hoeko
★ Ladismith

Zoar

Museum & Succulent Garden
Calitzdorp

Ladismith Klein Karoo
Nature Reserve ★

12

33° 29' 49" S
21° 15' 55" E

21

Boplaas ★
★★
Calitzdorp

R62

33° 35' 19" S
21° 10' 58" E

R62

4

33° 34' 02" S
21° 13' 22" E

ROOIBERG

81

Historic Churches

33° 31' 49" S
21° 41' 19" E

Remhoogte

37

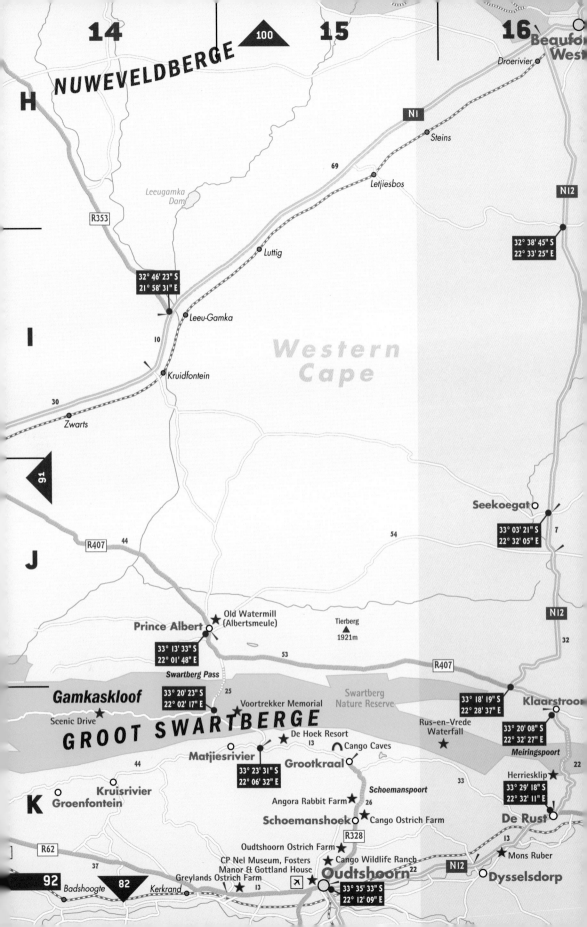

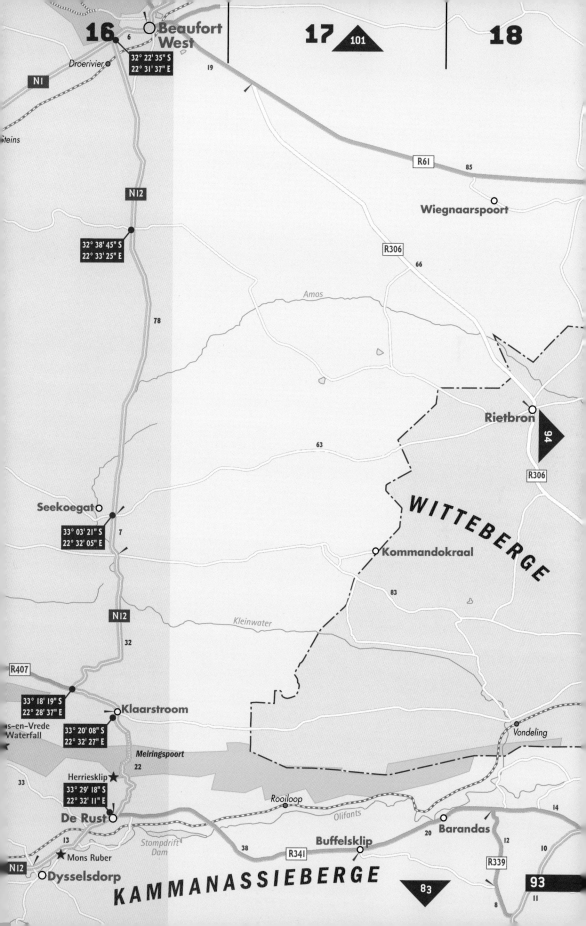

16 6 ○ **Beaufort West**

○ Droerivier

N1

32° 22' 35" S
22° 31' 37" E

19

101

R61 85

N12

32° 38' 45" S
22° 33' 25" E

○ **Wiegnaarspoort**

R306 66

Amos

78

63

R306

Rietbron ○

94

○ **Seekoegat** ●

33° 03' 21" S
22° 32' 05" E

7

WITTEBERGE

○ **Kommandokraal**

N12

83

32

Kleinwater

R407

33° 18' 19" S
22° 28' 37" E

○ **Klaarstroom** ●

33° 20' 08" S
22° 32' 27" E

s-en-Vrede
Waterfall

Meiringspoort

Vondeling ○

22

33

Herriesklip ★

33° 29' 18" S
22° 32' 11" E

Rooiloop

Olifants

14

De Rust ○

13

Stompdrift
Dam

38

R341

Buffelsklip ○

20 **Barandas** ○

12

10

R339

★ Mons Ruber

N12

○ **Dysselsdorp**

KAMMANASSIEBERGE

83

8 11

102

H

Uitky

44 R61

R61 85

Wiegnaarspoort

N9 51

I

Kaapse Poortjie

93

Rietbron

Sout

21

26

Beervlei
Dam

24

17

R306 44

23

Volstruisleegte

N9

Swanepoelspoo

27

WITTEBERGE

J

Perdepoort

Knoetze

▲ 1365m

19

R329

30

17

Willowmore

✈

**33° 18' 07" S
23° 28' 24" E**

BAVIAANSKLOOFBERGE

Vondeling

Ghwarriepoort

Buyspoort

41

43

15

Baviaansklo

K

14

Nuwekloof
Pass

45

12

**33° 30' 13" S
23° 13' 44" E**

10

R339

84

8

11

Zaaimansdal

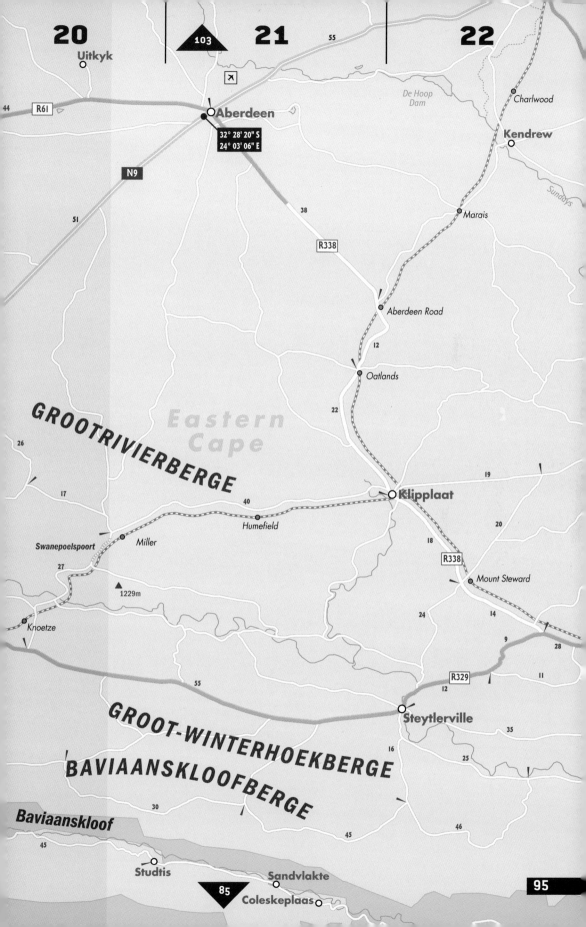

103

Uitkyk

✈

44 R61

Aberdeen

32° 28' 20" S
24° 03' 06" E

N9

De Hoop
Dam

Charlwood

Kendrew

51

38

Marais

R338

Sundays

Aberdeen Road

12

Oatlands

22

**Eastern
Cape**

19

GROOTRIVIERBERGE

26

17

40

Klipplaat

20

Humefield

Swanepoelspoort Miller

18

27

R338

▲ 1229m

Mount Steward

Knoetze

24

14

9

28

55

R329

11

12

Steytlerville

35

GROOT-WINTERHOEKBERGE

16

25

BAVIAANSKLOOFBERGE

30

Baviaanskloof

45

46

45

Studtis

Sandvlakte

▼ 85

Coleskeplaas

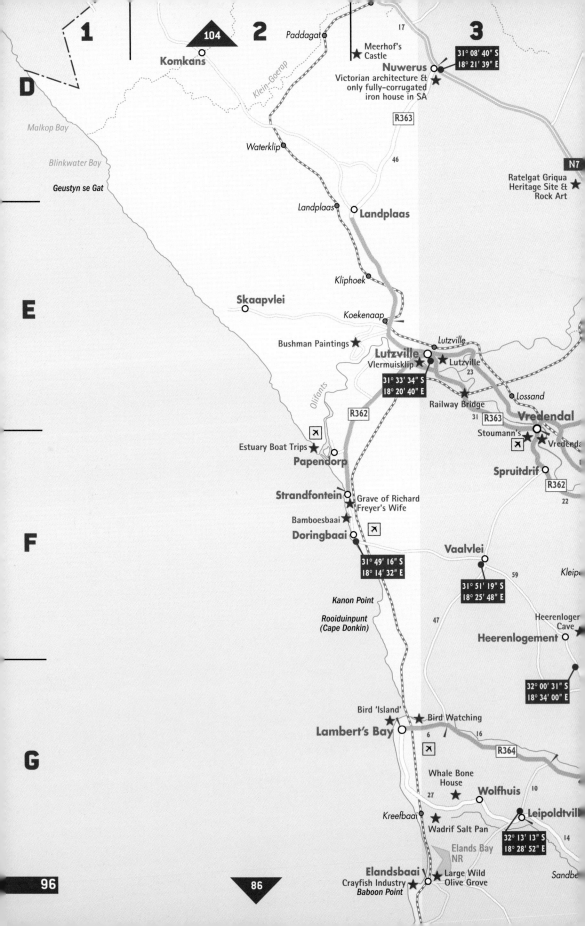

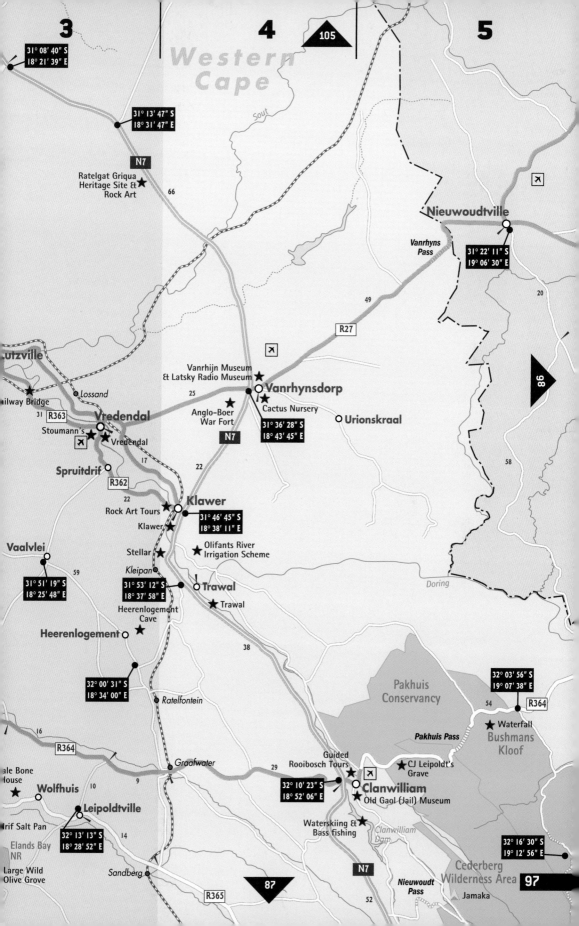

Western Cape

31° 08' 40" S
18° 21' 39" E

31° 13' 47" S
18° 31' 47" E

N7

Sout

66

Ratelgat Griqua
Heritage Site &
Rock Art

Nieuwoudtville

Vanrhyns
Pass

31° 22' 11" S
19° 06' 30" E

49

R27

20

86

58

Vanrhijn Museum
& Latsky Radio Museum

25

Vanrhynsdorp

Cactus Nursery

utzville

Lossand

ilway Bridge

31   R363

Vredendal

Stoumann's

Vredendal

Anglo-Boer
War Fort

Urionskraal

31° 36' 28" S
18° 43' 45" E

N7

Spruitdrif

17

R362

22

22

Klawer

Rock Art Tours

Klawer

31° 46' 45" S
18° 38' 11" E

Vaalvlei

Stellar

Olifants River
Irrigation Scheme

59

31° 51' 19" S
18° 25' 48" E

Kleipan

31° 53' 12" S
18° 37' 58" E

Trawal

Heerenlogement
Cave

Trawal

Doring

38

Heerenlogement

32° 00' 31" S
18° 34' 00" E

Ratelfontein

Pakhuis
Conservancy

32° 03' 56" S
19° 07' 38" E

54

R364

16

R364

Waterfall

Bushmans
Kloof

Pakhuis Pass

Graafwater

29

Guided
Rooibosch Tours

9

ale Bone
ouse

Wolfhuis

10

CJ Leipoldt's
Grave

32° 10' 23" S
18° 52' 06" E

Clanwilliam

Old Gaol (Jail) Museum

Leipoldtville

rif Salt Pan

Elands Bay
NR

Large Wild
Olive Grove

32° 13' 13" S
18° 28' 52" E

14

Waterskiing &
Bass fishing

Clanwilliam
Dam

32° 16' 30" S
19° 12' 56" E

Sandberg

N7

Nieuwoudt
Pass

Cederberg
Wilderness Area

Jamaka

R365

52

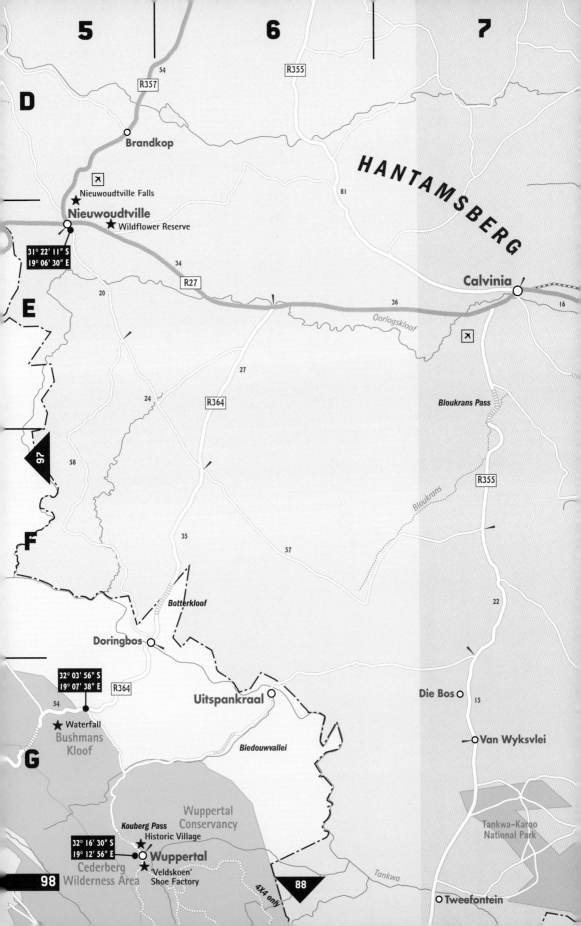

D

R357

54

Brandkop

✈

★ Nieuwoudtville Falls

Nieuwoudtville

★ Wildflower Reserve

31° 22' 11" S
19° 06' 30" E

HANTAMSBERG

81

Calvinia

16

34

R27

20

36

Oorlogskloof

E

27

24

R364

✈

Bloukrans Pass

97

58

R355

Bloukrans

F

35

57

22

Botterkloof

Doringbos

Die Bos

15

32° 03' 56" S
19° 07' 38" E

R364

54

Uitspankraal

Van Wyksvlei

★ Waterfall

Bushmans
Kloof

Biedouwvallei

G

Wuppertal
Conservancy

Tankwa-Karoo
National Park

Kouberg Pass

Historic Village

32° 16' 30" S
19° 12' 56" E

Wuppertal

98   Cederberg
Wilderness Area

★ 'Veldskoen'
Shoe Factory

4x4 only

88

Tankwa

Tweefontein

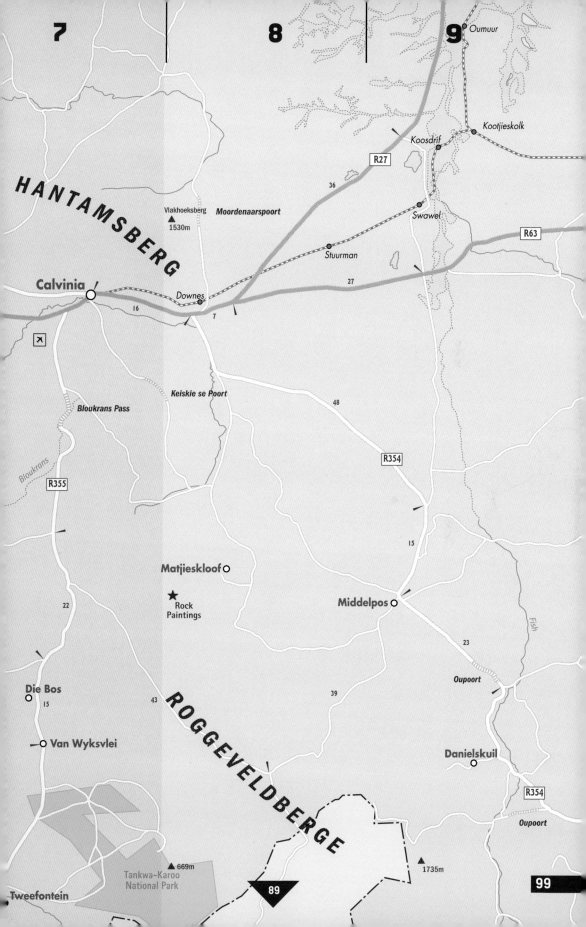

HANTAMSBERG

Oumuur

Kootjieskolk

Koosdrif

R27

36

Swawel

R63

Vlakhoeksberg
▲
1530m

Moordenaarspoort

Stuurman

27

Calvinia ○

Downes

16

7

✈

Keiskie se Poort

48

Bloukrans Pass

R354

Bloukrans

R355

15

Matjieskloof ○

★ Rock
Paintings

Middelpos ○

22

23

Oupoort

Die Bos
○
15

39

ROGGEVELDBERGE

43

○ Van Wyksvlei

Danielskuil
○

R354

Oupoort

▲ 669m

1735m
▲

Tankwa-Karoo
National Park

89

Fish

Tweefontein

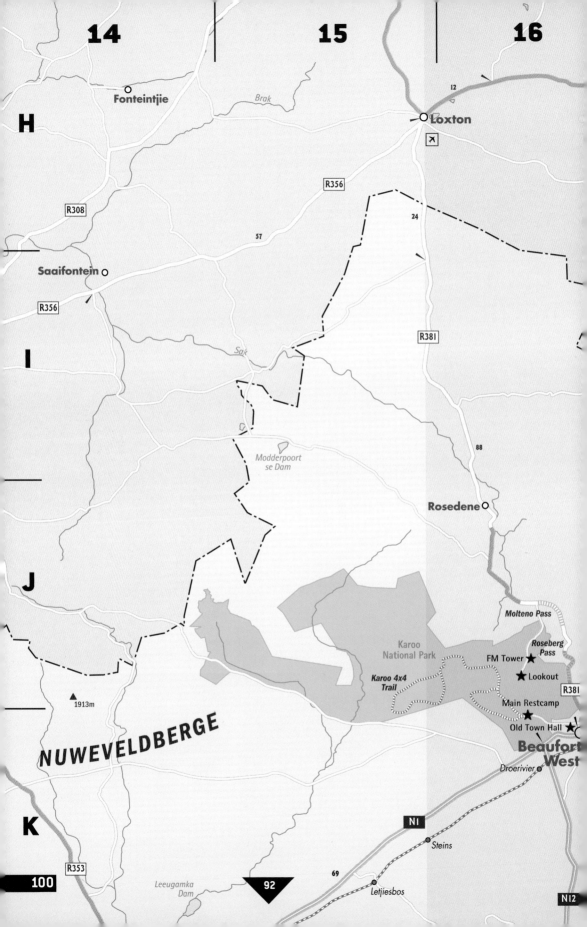

H

○ Fonteintjie

Brak

○ Loxton

12

R356

R308

57

○ Saaifontein

R356

I

Sak

R381

Modderpoort se Dam

88

Rosedene ○

J

Molteno Pass

Karoo National Park

Roseberg Pass

FM Tower ★

★ Lookout

Karoo 4x4 Trail

R381

Main Restcamp ★

▲ 1913m

Old Town Hall ★

NUWEVELDBERGE

Beaufort West

Droerivier ○

K

N1

○ Steins

R353

▼ 92

Leeugamka Dam

69

○ Letjiesbos

N12

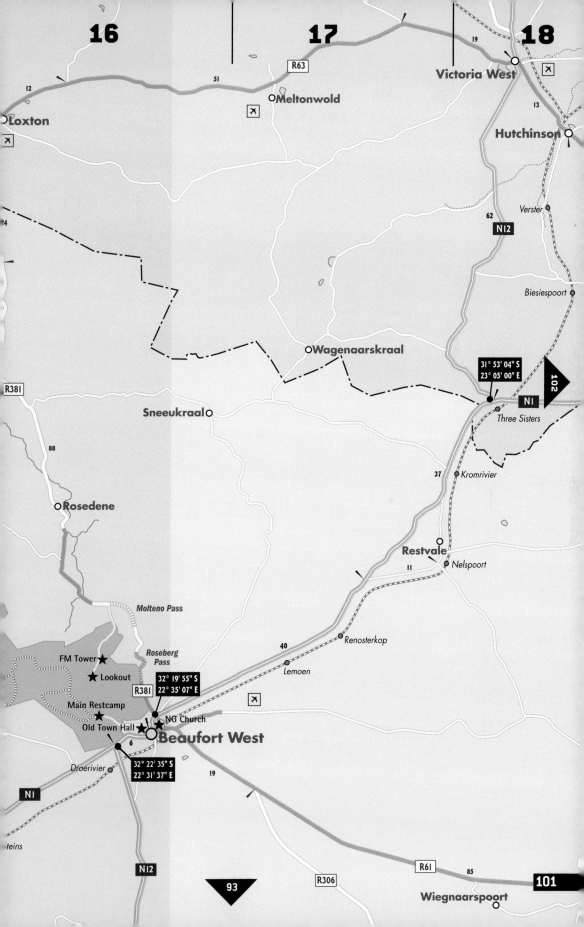

R63

◯Meltonwold

◯Loxton

12

51

19

Victoria West

✈

13

Hutchinson

Verster◯

62

N12

Biesiespoort◯

◯Wagenaarskraal

R381

R4

31° 53' 04" S
23° 05' 00" E

N1

102

Sneeukraal◯

Three Sisters

88

37

Kromrivier◯

◯Rosedene

Restvale

Nelspoort◯

11

Molteno Pass

40

Renosterkop◯

FM Tower ★

*Roseberg
Pass*

Lemoen◯

✈

★ Lookout

32° 19' 55" S
22° 35' 07" E

R381

Main Restcamp ★

NG Church

★★
Old Town Hall ★ ◯ **Beaufort West**

6

32° 22' 35" S
22° 31' 37" E

Droerivier◯

19

N1

teins

93

R306

R61

85

101

N12

Wiegnaarspoort

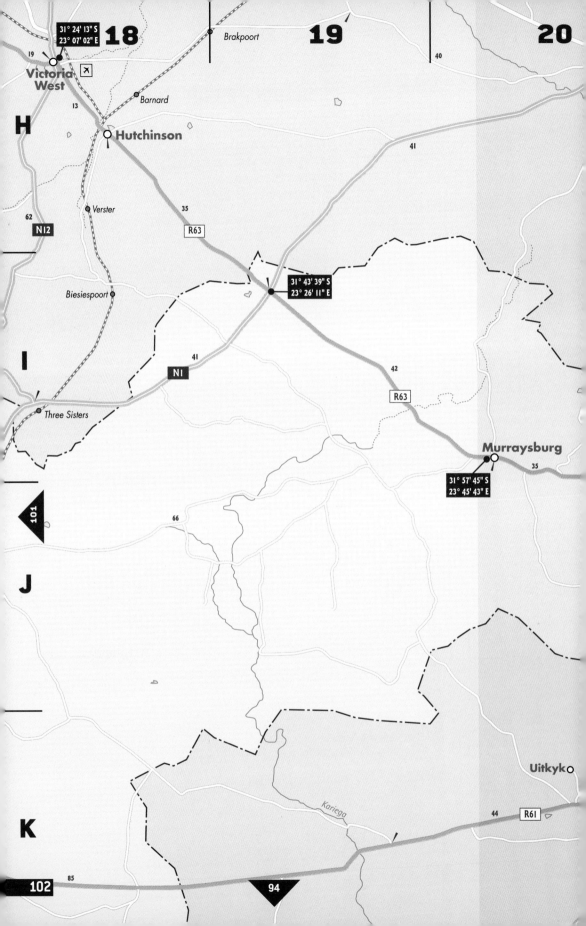

31° 24' 13" S
23° 07' 02" E

Brakpoort

19

40

19

Victoria
West

Barnard

13

H

Hutchinson

41

Verster

35

62

R63

N12

Biesiespoort

31° 43' 39" S
23° 26' 11" E

41

I

N1

42

R63

Three Sisters

Murraysburg

35

31° 57' 45" S
23° 45' 43" E

101

66

J

Uitkyk

Kariega

K

44

R61

102

85

94

Richmond

55

R398

72

Seekoei

S N E E U B E R G

Kranskop
▲
2052m

Driefontein

Nieu-Bethesda

Murraysburg

35

R63

55

55

Vanryneveldspas Dam

Oudeberg Pass

N9

Graaff-Reinet
32° 14' 59" S
24° 32' 06" E

★
Valley of Desolation
Munnikspoort

R75

Adendorp

55

Uitkyk

De Hoop
Dam

Charlwood

Sundays

R61

44

Aberdeen
32° 28' 20" S
24° 03' 06" E

Kendrew

N9

R338

▼ 95

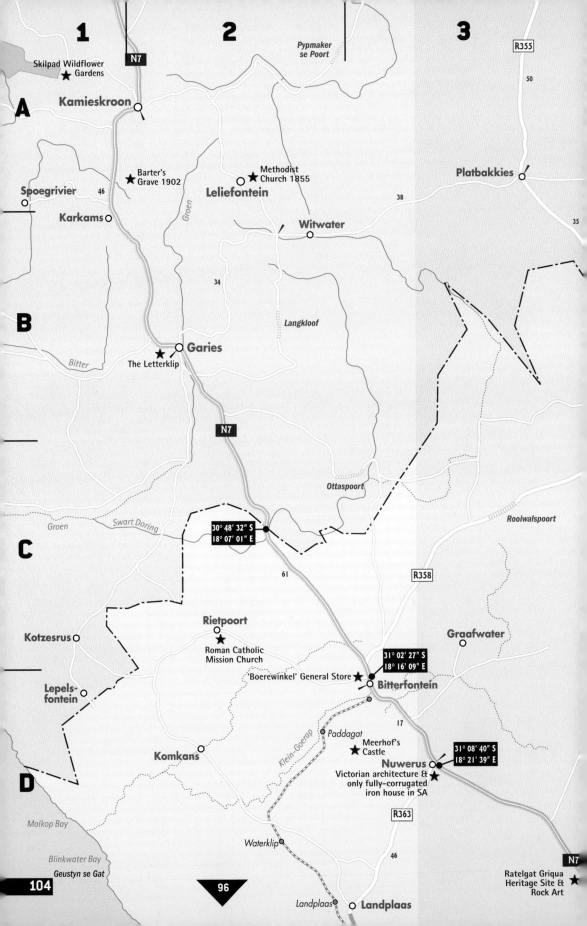

1

2

3

R355

Pypmaker
se Poort

N7

50

Skilpad Wildflower
★ Gardens

A   Kamieskroon ○

Barter's
★ Grave 1902

Methodist
★ Church 1855

Platbakkies ○

Spoegrivier   46
○

Leliefontein

38

Karkams ○

Groen

Witwater ⊢

35

34

B

Langkloof

Bitter

Garies ○   **Garies**
★
The Letterklip

N7

Ottaspoort

Groen   Swart Doring

30° 48' 32" S
18° 07' 01" E ●

Rooiwalspoort

C

61

R358

Rietpoort
★
Roman Catholic
Mission Church

Kotzesrus ○

Graafwater ○

31° 02' 27" S
18° 16' 09" E

'Boerewinkel' General Store ★ ●
Bitterfontein

Lepels-
fontein ○

17

Klein-Goerap

Paddagat ○
Meerhof's
★ Castle

31° 08' 40" S
18° 21' 39" E

Komkans ○

Nuwerus ●
★
Victorian architecture &
only fully-corrugated
iron house in SA

D

R363

Malkop Bay

46

Blinkwater Bay

N7

Geustyn se Gat

104

▼ **96**

Waterklip ○

Ratelgat Griqua
Heritage Site &
Rock Art ★

Landplaas ○   Landplaas ○

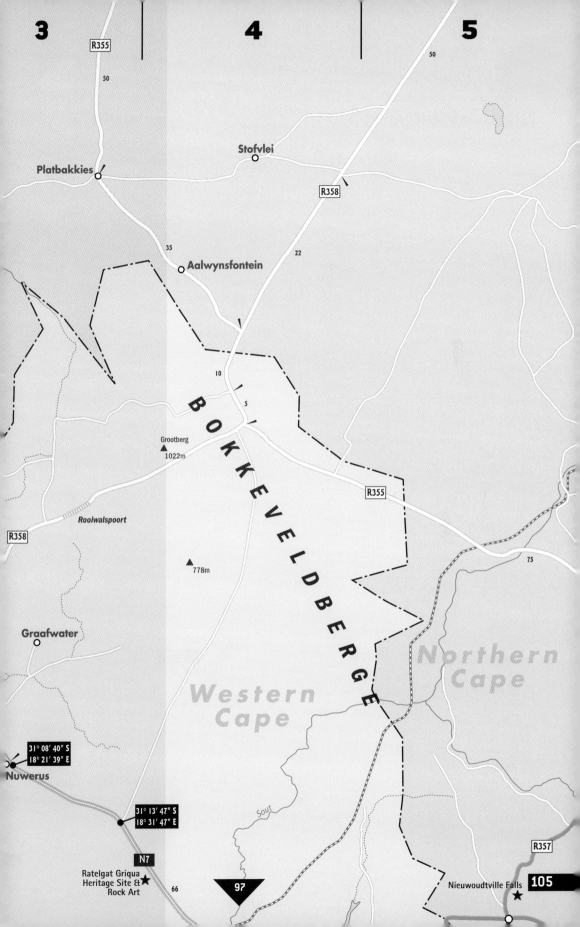

Map Index <small>pages 76-105</small>

NAME	GRID	PG	NAME	GRID	PG
			Cape Town	L3	76
PLACE NAMES INDEX			Cederberg	H6	88
Aalwynsfontein	B4	105	Ceres	K6	88
Abbotsdale	K4	87	Churchhaven	J2	86
Aberdeen	H21	95	Citrusdal	H5	87
Albertinia	M13	81	Clanwilliam	G5	97
Anysberg	K10	90	Clarkson	M22	85
Arniston	O9	79	Coleskeplaas	K21	95
Ashton	L8	79	Dana Bay	M14	82
Askraal	M11	80	Danielskuil	G9	99
Atlantis	K3	86	Darling	K3	86
Aurora	I3	86	Daskop	L17	83
Avondrust	K9	89	De Doorns	K7	88
Baardskeerdersbos	N7	78	De Hoek	I4	87
Barandas	K18	93	De Rust	K16	92
Barrington	L17	83	Die Bos	G7	98
Barrydale	L10	80	Die Dam	O7	78
Beaufort West	H16	92	Die Hel	K13	91
Bellville	L4	77	Die Vlug	L18	83
Bereaville	M6	78	Doringbaai	F2	96
Bergplaas	L16	83	Doringbos	F6	98
Bergrivier	I3	86	Droëvlakte	M12	81
Betty's Bay	N5	77	Durbanville	L4	77
Bitterfontein	D3	104	Dwarskersbos	I2	86
Blanco	L16	82	Dysselsdorp	K16	92
Bloubergstrand	L3	76	Eendekuil	I5	87
Bo-Wadrif	H8	89	Eight Bells	L14	82
Boerboonfontein	L10	80	Elandsbaai	G3	96
Bonnievale	L8	79	Elim	N7	78
Botrivier	M5	78	Fairfield	N7	78
Brandkop	D5	98	Faure	M4	77
Brandrivier	L11	80	Firgrove	M4	77
Bredasdorp	N8	79	Fish Hoek	M3	76
Buffelsbaai	M17	83	Franschhoek	L5	77
Buffelsdrif	L17	83	Gansbaai	N6	78
Buffelsklip	K17	93	Gansfontein	I7	88
Caledon	M6	78	Garies	B2	104
Calitzdorp	K13	91	Genadendal	M7	78
Calvinia	E7	98	George	L16	82
Cambria	L22	85	Glentana	M15	82

Map Index

NAME	GRID	PG	NAME	GRID	PG
Gordon's Bay	M4	77	Kleinbaai	N6	78
Gouda	J5	87	Kleinmond	N5	77
Gouna	L18	83	Kleinplaat	L16	83
Gouritsmond	N14	82	Knysna	M18	83
Graafwater	C3	104	Komkans	D2	104
Grabouw	M5	77	Kommandokraal	J17	93
Greyton	M7	78	Kommetjie	M3	76
Groendal	L5	77	Koringplaas	I11	90
Groenfontein	K14	92	Kotzesrus	C1	104
Groot Brakrivier	M15	82	Koutjie	L16	83
Groot Jongensfontein	N12	81	Kruisrivier	K14	92
Grootkraal	K15	92	Kuilsrivier	L4	77
Haarlem	L18	84	Kylemore	L5	77
Hammanshof	L6	78	L'Agulhas	O8	79
Harkerville	M18	84	Laaiplek	I2	86
Hartenbos	M15	82	Ladismith	K12	91
Hawston	N5	77	Laingsburg	J11	90
Heerenlogement	F3	96	Lambert's Bay	G3	96
Heidelberg	M11	80	Landplaas	E3	96
Herbertsdale	M14	81	Langberg	L13	81
Hermanus	N6	78	Langebaan	J2	86
Herold	L16	83	Langebaanweg	I2	86
Herolds Bay	M16	82	Leipoldtville	G3	96
Hilandale	J10	90	Leliefontein	A2	104
Hoeko	K12	91	Lepelsfontein	D1	104
Hopefield	J3	86	Lindeshof	M7	78
Hotagterklip	O8	79	Llandudno	M3	76
Hottentotskloof	J7	88	Lutzville	E3	96
Hout Bay	M3	76	Malgas	N10	80
Infanta	N11	80	Malmesbury	K4	87
Johnson's Post	M14	82	Mamre	K3	86
Joubertina	L20	84	Matjieskloof	F8	99
Kamieskroon	A2	104	Matjiesrivier	K15	92
Karatara	L17	83	McGregor	L7	78
Kareedouw	L21	85	Melkbosstrand	L3	76
Kareevlakte	K10	90	Merweville	I13	91
Karkams	B1	104	Middelpos	F9	99
Kendrew	H22	95	Milnerton	L3	76
Klaarstroom	K16	92	Molenrivier	L17	83
Klawer	F4	97	Montagu	L8	79

Map Index pages 76-105

Map Index

NAME	GRID	PG
Touws River	K8	89
Trawal	F4	97
Tulbagh	J5	87
Tweefontein	H7	98
Uitkyk	H20	94
Uitspankraal	G6	98
Uniondale	L18	83
Urionskraal	E4	97
Vaalvlei	F3	96
Van Wyksdorp	L13	81
Van Wyksvlei	G7	98
Vanrhynsdorp	E4	97
Velddrif	I2	86
Vermaaklikheid	N11	80
Victoria Bay	M16	82
Villiersdorp	M6	78
Vlees Bay	M14	82
Vleiland	K12	91
Volstruisleegte	J19	94
Vredenburg	I2	86
Vredendal	E3	96
Wellington	L5	77
Wiegnaarspoort	H18	93
Wilderness	M16	83
Willowmore	J19	94
Windmill	L5	77
Witsand	N11	80
Wittedrift	M18	84
Wittewater	I4	87
Witwater	B2	104
Wolfhuis	G3	96
Wolseley	K5	88
Woodlands	M21	85
Worcester	L6	78
Wuppertal	G6	98
Wydgeleë	N9	79
Yzerfontein	K2	86
Zaaimansdal	K19	94
Zoar	K13	91

Resources

WESTERN CAPE CONTACT DETAILS & INFORMATION

The following telephone numbers (and cyber connections) are correct at time of going to print. Numbers and codes do change over time, as do the names of establishments. For any queries dial 1023 (telephone enquiries), 10118 (the Talking Yellow Pages) or visit www.yellowpages.co.za (the electronic yellow pages). NOTE: numbers listed are all phone numbers – no fax numbers or physical addresses are provided here.

EMERGENCIES
- Ambulance 10177
- Fire and other emergencies 107
- Automobile Association Emergency 0800 111 998

GENERAL
- South Africa online: www.southafrica.net
- Cape Town & Western Cape Tourism
  021 418 5202
  info@tourismcapetown.co.za
  www.tourismcapetown.co.za
- Cape Town Tourism
  086 132 2223
  info@capetown.travel
  www.capetown.travel
- Weather Bureau 082 162
- Cape Town International Airport 021 937 1200
- George Airport 044 876 9310

TRANSPORT
- Automobile Association 0800 111 997

- Transnet Freight Rail
  086 000 8888
- Blue Train 021 449 2672
- Metrorail 0800 65 64 63

BUS SERVICES
- Baz Bus 021 422 5202
- Greyhound 021 418 4326/ 083 915 9000
- Intercape 0861 28 72 87/ 021 380 4400
- MyCiti 0800 65 64 63 http://myciti.org.za/
- Translux 0861 589 282

CAR RENTAL
- Avis 0861 02 11 11 www.avis.co.za
- Budget 0861 01 66 22 www.budget.co.za
- Europcar (Imperial) 0861 13 10 00 www.europcar.co.za
- Tempest 0861 836 7378 www.tempestcarhire.co.za
- First Car Rental 0861 011 323

ACCOMMODATION
- City Lodge 0800 11 37 90
- Holiday Inn 0800 999 136
- Protea Hotels 0861 11 90 00
- Southern Sun 0861 447 744

AIRLINES
- British Airways 021 936 9000
- KLM 0860 24 77 47
- Kulula.com 0861 58 58 52
- Mango Airlines 021 936 2848/ 0861 162 646
- South African Airways 021 936 1111/0861 359 722

MONEY MATTERS
- ABSA 0800 111 155
- American Express 0800 110 929

- Capitec Bank 0860 102 043
- Diners Club 0860 34 63 77
- First National Bank 0800 110 132
- Mastercard 0800 990 418
- Nedbank 0800 110 929
- Rennies Foreign Exchange (Thomas Cook) 0860 11 11 77
- Standard Bank 0800 020 600
- VISA 0800 990 475

CELLPHONE PROVIDERS
- Cell C 0861 80 04 00/084 140
- Virgin Mobile 0741 00 01 23
- MTN 083 18 08
- Vodacom 082 111

ENTERTAINMENT
- Artscape Theatre Centre 021 421 7695
- Baxter Theatre Centre 021 685 7880
- Computicket 083 915 8000
- Nu-Metro 0861 24 63 62
- On Broadway 021 424 1194
- Ster-Kinekor 082 167 89

CAPE TOWN
- Cape Town Tourism
  086 132 2223
  info@capetown.travel
  www.capetown.travel
- Cape Town Inernational Airport International Arrivals Visitor Information Kiosk 021 935 3160 airport@capetown.travel
- Cape Town International Airport Domestic Arrivals Visitor Information Kiosk 021 935 6060 airport2@capetown.travel

CAPE TOWN CITY BOWL & ENVIRONS
- Cape Town Holocaust Centre 021 462 5553

Resources

- Cape Town International
  Convention Centre
  021 410 5000
- Castle of Good Hope
  021 787 1260
- District Six Museum
  021 466 7200
- Iziko SA Museum 021 481 3800
- Iziko South African National
  Gallery 021 467 4660
- Mount Nelson Hotel
  021 483 1000
- Planetarium 021 481 3900
- Robben Island Museum
  (Nelson Mandela Gateway)
  021 413 4220/1
- St George's Cathedral
  021 424 7360
- Table Mountain Aerial Cableway
  021 424 8181
- Cape Town Tourism (Table
  Mountain Lower Cableway)
  021 422 1075
  tablemountain@capetown.travel
- Two Oceans Aquarium
  021 418 3823
- Cape Town Tourism
  (V&A Waterfront)
  021 408 7600
  info@waterfront.co.za
- V&A Waterfront 021 408 7600

THE CAPE PENINSULA & NORTHERN SUBURBS
- Blaauwberg Tourism Office
  021 521 1080
  blaauwberg@capetown.travel
  www.capetown.travel
- Cape of Good Hope Gate
  (Table Mountain National Park)
  021 780 9526
- Table Mountain National Park
  021 701 8692
- Cape Point Ostrich Farm
  021 780 9294

- Grass Roots 021 706 1006
- Ilios Travel 021 697 4056
  resteam@ilios.co.za
  www.ilios.co.za
- Two Oceans Restaurant
  021 780 9200
- CitySightseeing Cape Town
  021 511 6000
  info@citysightseeing.co.za
  www.citysightseeing.co.za

Camps Bay
- Bay Hotel 021 438 4444/
  021 437 9701 (Bookings)
- Blues Restaurant 021 438 2040
- Theatre on the Bay 021 438 3301

Constantia
- Buitenverwachting 021 794 5191
- Constantia Uitsig 021 794 6500
- Constantia Village 021 794 5065
- Groot Constantia 021 794 5128
- Klein Constantia 021 794 5188
- Jonkershuis Restaurant
  021 794 6255
- Steenberg Estate 021 713 2211

Durbanville (Tygerberg)
- Altydgedacht 021 976 1295
- Bloemendal Wines 021 976 2682
- Diemersdal Wines 021 976 3361
- Durbanville Hills Wines
  021 558 1300
- GrandWest Casino 021 505 7777
- Meerendal Estate 021 975 1655
- N1 City Shopping Centre
  021 595 1170
- Nitida Estate 021 976 1467
- Tygerberg Nature Reserve
  021 913 5695
- Tyger Valley Shopping Centre
  021 914 1822
- Willowbridge 021 915 4080,
  willowbridge@capetown.travel

Fish Hoek
- Simon's Town 021 786 8440,
  simonstown@capetown.travel

Hout Bay
- Chapman's Peak Hotel
  021 790 1036
- Mariner's Wharf 021 790 1100
- Hout Bay Visitor Information
  Centre 021 791 8380
  houtbay@capetown.travel
- World of Birds 021 790 2730

Kalk Bay
- Cape to Cuba 021 788 1566
- Olympia Cafe 021 788 6396

Kommetjie
- Imhoff Farm 021 783 4545
- Noordhoek 021 789 2812
  info@noordhoektourism.co.za

Melkbosstrand / Milnerton
- Canal Walk Shopping Centre
  021 529 9699/8
- Koeberg Nuclear Power Station
  Visitors Centre 021 550 4667
- Cape Town Tourism (Canal Walk)
  021 555 3100
  visitorinfo@canalwalk.co.za
- Ratanga Junction 0861 200 300

Muizenberg
- Muizenberg 021 787 9140,
  muizenberg@capetown.travel

Newlands
- Cavendish Square Shopping
  Centre
  021 657 5620
- Kirstenbosch National Botanical
  Garden
  021 799 8783
- South African Breweries
  021 658 7511

Resources

Noordhoek
- Noordhoek 021 789 2812
  info@noordhoektourism.co.za

Simon's Town
- Boulders Beach (Table Mountain National Park) 021 786 2329
- Simon's Town 021 786 8440, simonstown@capetown.travel
- Simon's Town Museum 021 786 3046
- South African Naval Base 021 787 3911
- Warrior Toy Museum 021 786 1395

THE WINELANDS
- Winelands Tourist Information 0861 265 263
  info@bolandm.co.za
  www.tourismcapewinelands.co.za

Gordon's Bay, Strand & Somerset West
- Somerset West 021 840 1400
  somersetwest@capetown.travel
- Cape Town Tourism (Strand) 021 853 1688
  strand@capetown.travel
- Cape Town Tourism (Gordon's Bay) 021 856 1444
  gordonsbay@capetown.travel
- Monkey Town 021 858 1060
- Somerset Mall Shopping Centre 021 852 7114
- Vergelegen 021 847 1334

Franschhoek
- Boschendal Estate 021 870 4200
- Haute Cabrière 021 876 8500
- Franschhoek Tourism Bureau 021 876 3603
  info@franschhoek.org.za
  www.franschhoek.org.za

- Huguenot Museum 021 876 2532
- La Motte 021 876 3114
- La Petite Ferme 021 876 3016
- Môreson Estate 021 876 3055,3692

Paarl
- Afrikaans Language Museum 021 872 3441
- Butterfly World 021 875 5628
- La Bonheur Crocodile Farm 021 863 1142
- Fairview Wine Estate 021 863 2450
- KWV (HO & Wine Emporium) 021 807 3007
- Nederburg 021 862 3104
- Paarl Museum 021 872 2651
- Paarl Tourism Bureau 021 872 0860
  info@paarlonline.com
  www.paarlonline.com

Stellenbosch
- Bergkelder 021 809 8025
- Delheim Wine Estate 021 888 4600
- Historical Walks 021 883 9633
- Morgenhof 021 889 5510
- Oom Samie se Winkel 021 887 0797
- Spier 021 8091100
- Stellenbosch Information Office 021 883 3584
  info@stellenboschtourism.co.za
  www.tourismstellenbosch.co.za
- Stellenbosch Museum 021 887 2902
- Stellenbosch Wine Route 021 886 4310
- Van Rhyn Brandy Cellars 021 881 3875

Wellington
- Hottentots Holland Nature Reserve 028 841 4826
- Bokomo Foods 021 864 8690
- Wellington Museum 021 873 4710
- Wellington Wine Route & Tourism 021 873 4604

WEST COAST, OVERBERG, KAROO AND GARDEN ROUTE
- Breede Valley Tourism 023 348 2795
  jcdamens@breedevallei.gov.za
- Central Karoo Regional Tourism Office 023 449 1000
  jjonkers@skdm.co.za
  www.tourismcentralkaroo.co.za
- The Garden Route Klein Karoo Regional Tourism Organization 044 873 6314
  info@gardenroute.org.za
  www.tourismcapegardenroute.co.za
- Hex Valley Tourism 023 356 2041
  hvtourism@telkomsa.net
  www.hexrivervalley.co.za
- Overberg Tourism 028 425 1157
  info@capeoverberg.org
  www.tourismcapeoverberg.org
- West Coast Regional Tourism 022 433 8505
  tourism@wcdm.co.za
  www.tourismcapewestcoast.co.za

Arniston
- Arniston Hotel 028 445 9000
- Tourist Info 028 424 2584
  suidpunt@brd.dorea.co.za
  www.tourismcapeagulhas.co.za

Barrydale
- Tourist Info 028 572 1572
  info@barrydale.co.za
  www.barrydale.co.za

Beaufort West
- Karoo National Park
  023 415 2828
- Beaufort West Tourism
  023 415 1488
  bwtbinfo@xsinet.co.za
  www.tourismbeaufortwest.co.za
  Bredasdorp
- De Hoop Nature Reserve
  028 542 1253
- Tourist Info 028 424 2584
  suidpunt@brd.dorea.co.za
  www.tourismcapeagulhas.co.za
- Bredasdorp Museum
  028 424 1240

Caledon
- Caledon Hotel 028 214 5100
- Tourist Info 028 212 3282
  calmuse@intekom.co.za
  www.tourismcaledon.co.za

Ceres
- The Fruit Route 023 316 1287
- Kagga Kamma Nature Reserve
  021 872 4343
- Matroosberg Reserve
  023 312 2282
- Togryers Museum
  (Transport Riders' Museum)
  023 312 2045
- Tourist Info 023 316 1287
  info@ceres.org.za, www.ceres.
  org.za
  www.tourismceres.co.za

Citrusdal
- Tourist Info 022 921 3210,
  info@citrusdal.info
  www.citrusdal.info
  www.tourismcitrusdal.co.za

Clanwilliam
- Cederberg Wines 027 482 2827
- Cederberg Wilderness Area &
  Nature Reserve 027 482 2812
- Die Kunshuis Art Gallery
  027 482 1940
- Rooibos Ltd – Tea & Natural
  Products 027 482 2155
  www.rooibosltd.co.za
- Tourist Info 027 482 2024
  cederberg@lando.co.za
  www.clanwilliam.info
  www.tourismclanwilliam.co.za

Darling
- Evita se Perron
  022 492 2831/2851
- Rondeberg Nature Reserve
  022 492 3435
- Tourist Info 022 492 3361
  info@darlingtourism.co.za
  www.darlingtourism.co.za
- Wild Flower Line 022 492 3361,
  083 910 1028

Dwarskersbos
- Tourist Info 022 783 1821

Eland's Bay
- Crayfish permits at the Post
  Office 022 972 1700
- Tourist Info 022 972 1640
  info@elandsbayhotel.co.za
  www.elandsbayhotel.co.za

Elgin / Grabouw
- Elgin Valley Tourism Bureau
  021 848 9838
  info@elginvalley.co.za
  www.elginvalley.co.za
- Elgin Apple Museum
  021 848 9060
- Paul Cluver Amphitheatre
  021 844 0605

Elim
- Tourist Info 028 482 1806,
  084 974 8731

George
- George Museum 044 873 5343
- Fancourt Hotel and Country Club
  044 804 0010
- Outeniqua Nature Reserve
  044 870 8323/5
- Outeniqua Railway Museum
  044 801 8288
- Tourist Info 044 801 9103
  info@georgetourism.co.za
  www.visitgeorge.co.za

Greyton
- Greyton Lodge
  028 254 9876/9800
- Greyton Nature Reserve
  028 254 9414
- Tourist Info 028 254 9414/9564
  greytoninfo@mweb.co.za
  www.greyton.net

Hermanus
- Bouchard Finlayson Vineyards
  028 312 3515
- Hamilton Russell Vineyards
  028 312 3595
- Hermanus Whale Hotline
  028 312 2629
- Old Harbour Museum
  028 312 1475
- Tourist Info 028 312 2629
  infoburo@hermanus.co.za
  www.tourismhermanus.co.za

Hopefield
- Tourist Info 022 723 1720

Jacobsbaai
- Tourist Info 022 714 2088
  sbto@saldanha.co.za
  www.tourismsaldanhabay.co.za

Resources

Kleinplasie
- Kleinplasie Living Open Air
  Museum
  023 342 2225/6

Kleinmond
- Tourist Info 028 271 5657
  info@ecoscape.org.za
  www.ecoscape.org.za

Knysna
- Featherbed Nature Reserve
  044 382 1693
- Knysna Forest 044 382 5466
- Knysna Oyster Co.
  044 382 6941/2
- Knysna Quays Waterfront
  044 382 0955
- Mitchell's Brewery 044 382 4685
- Nature's Valley 044 531 6700
- Tourist Info 044 382 5510
  info@knysna_info.co.za
  www.visitknysna.co.za

Laingsburg
- Tourist Info 023 551 1868
  laingsburg@xsinet.co.za
  www.tourismcentralkaroo.co.za

Lambert's Bay
- Tourist Info 027 432 1000
  lambertsinfo@mweb.co.za
  www.tourismlambertsbay.co.za

Langebaan
- Club Mykonos 022 707 7000
- Die Strandloper 022 772 2490
- Postberg Nature Reserve
  022 772 2144
- Tourist Info 022 772 1515
  langebaan@sbto.co.za
  www.tourismlangebaan.co.za
- West Coast Fossil Park
  022 766 1606

West Coast National Park
- West Coast National Park
  022 772 2144
- Wild Flower line 022 772 1515

Malmesbury
- Sasko Grain (Bokomo Mills)
  022 482 7272
- Malmesbury Museum
  022 482 2332
- Swartland Wine Route
  022 487 1133
  swartlandinfo@westc.co.za
  www.swartlandwineroute.co.za
- Tourist Info 022 487 1133
  swartlandtourism@westc.co.za
  www.tourismswartland.co.za

Matjiesfontein
- Lord Milner Hotel 023 561 3011

McGregor
- Tourist Info 023 625 1671
  info@tourismmcgregor.co.za
  www.tourismmcgregor.co.za
- Vrolijkheid Nature Reserve
  023 625 1621

Montagu
- Montagu Hot Mineral Springs
  023 614 1050
- Montagu Museum 023 614 1950
- Tourist Info 023 614 2471
  info@montagu-ashton.info
  www.montagu.org.za

Mossel Bay
- Tourist Info 044 691 2202
  marketing@visitmosselbay.co.za
  www.visitmosselbay.co.za

Oudtshoorn
- CP Nel Museum 044 272 7306
- Cango Caves 044 272 7410
- Cango Ostrich Farm
  044 272 4623

Cango Wildlife Ranch
- Cango Wildlife Ranch
  044 272 5593
- Swartberg Nature Reserve and
  Pass 044 203 6325
- Tourist Info 044 279 2532
  otb@mweb.co.za
  www.tourismoudtshoorn.co.za

Paternoster
- Cape Columbine Lighthouse
  022 752 2705
- Columbine Nature Reserve
  022 752 2718
- Tourist Info 022 752 2323
  info@paternoster.info

Piketberg
- Historic Watermill
  022 913 1947
- Piketberg Museum 022 913 1126
- Tourist Info 022 913 2063
  tourism@piketberg.com
  www.tourismpiketberg.co.za
- Winkelshoek Wine Cellar
  022 913 1092

Plettenberg Bay
- Goukamma Nature Reserve
  044 383 0042
- Nature Conservation &
  Reserves 044 802 5310
- Tourist Info 044 533 4065
  info@plettenbergbay.co.za
  www.plettenbergbay.co.za
  www.tourismplettenbergbay.
  co.za

Porterville
- Groot Winterhoek Nature Reserve
  022 931 2088
- Tourist Info 022 931 3732
  info@portervilletourism.co.za
  www.portervilletourism.co.za

Resources

Port Owen
- Port Owen Marina 022 783 1144
- Tourist Info 022 783 1821

Prince Albert
- Tourist Info 023 541 1366
  princealberttourism@intekom.
  co.za
  www.patourism.co.za

Robertson
- Dassieshoek Nature Reserve
  023 615 8000/8038
- De Wetshof Wine Cellars
  023 615 1853
- Graham Beck 023 626 1214
- Robertson Museum
  023 626 3681
- Robertson Wine Valley
  023 626 3167
- Soekershof (world's largest
  maze) 023 626 4134
- Tourist Info 023 626 4437
  info@robertson.org
  www.tourismrobertson.co.za

Saldanha
- SAS Saldanha Nature Reserve
  022 702 3523
- Tourist Info 022 714 2088
  sbto@saldanhabay.co.za
  www.sbto.co.za
  www.tourismsaldanhabay.co.za

Sedgefield
- Goukamma Nature Reserve
  044 383 0042
- Tourist Info 044 343 2658
  sedgefield@knysna_info.co.za
  www.tourismsedgefield.co.za

St Helena
- Tourist Info 022 715 1142
- Vasco da Gama Nautical Museum
  022 742 1906/1199

Still Bay/Stilbaai
- Tourist Info 028 754 2602
  stilbaai@hessequa.net
  www.tourismstilbaai.co.za

Swellendam
- Bontebok National Park
  028 514 2735
- Wildebraam Liqueur Farm
  028 514 3132
- The Drostdy Museum
  028 514 1138
- Marloth Nature Reserve
  028 514 1410
- Tourist Info 028 514 8580
  marketing.sto@vodamail.co.za
  www.swellendamtourism.co.za

Tulbagh
- Tourist Info 023 230 1348/1375
  tulbaghinfo@lando.co.za
  www.tourismtulbagh.co.za

Vanrhynsdorp
- Kokerboom Succulent Nursery
  027 219 1062
- Latsky Radio Museum
  027 219 1032
- Gifberg Holiday Resort
  027 219 1555
- Tourist Info 027 219 1552
  matzikamatourism@gmail.com
  www.tourismvanrhynsdorp.co.za

Velddrif
- Tourist Info 022 783 1821
  velddriftoerisme@telkomsa.net
  www.tourismvelddrif.co.za

Vredenburg
- Vredenburg Golf Course
  022 715 3003
- Tourist Info 022 715 1142
  vredenburg@sbto.co.za

Vredendal
- Matzikama Eco Park
  027 213 3794
- Spuitdrift Wine Cellar
  027 213 3086
- Tourist Info 027 201 3376
  matzikamatourism@gmail.com
- Vredendal Co-op 027 213 1080

Wilderness
- George/Wilderness Tourism
  044 877 0045
  weta@wildernessinfo.co.za
  www.tourismwilderness.co.za

Witsand
- Tourist Info 028 537 1010
  wact@telkomsa.net
  www.tourismwitsand.co.za

Worcester
- Karoo National Botanic Garden
  023 347 0785
- Tourist Info 023 348 2795
  www.tourismworcester.co.za

Wupperthal
- Tourist Info 027 492 3410
  www.tourismwupperthal.co.za

Yzerfontein
- Tourist Info 022 451 2366
  yzerfontein@polka.co.za
  www.tourismyzerfontein.
  co.za

✈ AIRPORT   ✕ AIRFIELD

CITIES & TOWNS

CAPE TOWN   CAPITAL CITY   CAPE TOWN

⊙ Paarl   MAJOR TOWN   ⊙ Paarl

○ Caledon   TOWN   ◉ Caledon

○ Franschhoek   LARGE VILLAGE   ⊙ Franschhoek

○ Llandudno   VILLAGE   ○ Llandudno

ROAD & OTHER CLASSIFICATIONS

N1	NATIONAL MAJOR / CONNECTING ROAD
	OTHER MAJOR / CONNECTING ROAD
R310	MAIN ROAD TARRED / ROUTE NUMBER
○	MAIN ROAD UNTARRED / INTERCHANGE
	MINOR ROAD TARRED
	MINOR ROAD UNTARRED
	4WD / 4X4 ROAD UNTARRED
	OTHER ROAD
	SCENIC ROUTE

TOWN PLAN ROADS

	MAJOR ROADS
	MAIN ROADS
	OTHER ROADS
Shaws Pass ●●●●	PASS SYMBOL
●●●●	RAILWAY LINE
24 ⏐ ⟋ 12	DISTANCE & PIN

SYMBOLS FOR TOWN PLANS

◉ ⬚ POLICE / PARK & SERVICE GATE

Ⓗ Ⓐ HOTEL & OTHER ACCOMMODATION

⌂ RESTCAMP / CAMPSITE [STATE RUN]

⌂ CAMP & LODGE [INCLUDES OTHER ACCOMMODATION]

△ ⬚ CAMPING & TENT FACILITIES / CARAVAN PARK

✚ HOSPITAL & CLINIC

✝ PLACE OF WORSHIP

⬚ WINE FARM / ESTATES

ⓘ ✉ INFORMATION OFFICE / POST OFFICE

🐋 🐦 WHALE / BIRD WATCHING

🚶 🏊 🤿 HIKING / SWIMMING / DIVING

🚨 LIGHTHOUSE / SHIPWRECK

PLACE OF INTEREST SYMBOLS

○ POINT OF INTEREST

◎ BUILDING - BANK ETC

○ SHOP

▲ 350m Signal Hill   PEAK SYMBOL & HEIGHT

⟵ TO CAPE TOWN

⟵ **To Cape Town**   TOWN PLAN & REGIONAL DIRECTIONAL

– – – – – INTERNATIONAL BOUNDARY

Table Mountain National Park	PARK FILL & NATURE RESERVE	🌲 Table Mountain National Park
	BUILT UP	LAKE & DAM
〰️		LARGE RIVER
		RIVER & COASTLINE
┄┄┄		DRY RIVER
☁	▭	PAN / WATERFALL

Top Statistics

FIRSTS FOR THE WESTERN CAPE

FOOTSTEPS 117 000 years ago the first recorded homo sapien footprints were left near the Langebaan Lagoon.

VINE In 1659 the vines Jan van Riebeeck had planted produced their first wine.

WINE In 1925 Abraham Perold (a professor at Stellenbosch University) developed the unique cultivar, Pinotage.

HEART In 1967 Professor Chris Barnard completed the world's first heart transplant at Groote Schuur hospital in Cape Town.

TRAVEL In 1492 Vasco da Gama became the first man to round the Cape of Good Hope ... and in so doing discovered the route to India.

LANDING In 1488 Bartolomeu Dias landed at Mossel Bay ... the first recorded European presence in South Africa.

BUILDING Between 1666 and 1679 South Africa's oldest surviving building was put up ... The Castle of Good Hope in Cape Town.

SACRIFICE The *HMS Birkenhead* sank off Gansbaai in February 1852; the tragedy is remembered as it was the first time the famous words "women and children first" were used.

SPACE The first South African (and second African) in space was billionaire internet entrepreneur Mark Shuttleworth (who was schooled and lived in Cape Town), who paid for his seat in 2002 and conducted valuable scientific research on board the international space station.

SIZE MATTERS

(the Western Cape's longest, shortest, slowest, rarest ...).

The highest bungi-jump in the world is at Bloukrans Bungy Jump Point, on the Garden Route. The brave enjoy a drop of 216m (708ft).

KWV in Paarl boasts the world's biggest wine cellar as well as the largest wine barrels on earth.

Malgas has South Africa's only remaining hand-drawn pont, which draws visitors across the Breede River.

Cape Town housewife Susan Rosenkowitz is mother of the world's oldest surviving sextuplets: her three boys and three girls were born in Cape Town on 11 January 1974.

The Western Cape boasts the longest wine route in the world, running along Route 62 from Paarl to the Klein Karoo.

Cape Town apparently boasts one of the world's highest ratios of women to men (3:1), although some claim that this statistic is a bit 'bent'.

Sea Point (a coastal suburb in Cape Town) is on record as having the world's greatest concentration of restaurants.

Construction of South Africa's first nuclear power station (at Koeberg in Cape Town) began in 1976.

The annual Cape Argus/Pick n Pay Cycle Tour is the largest timed cycle race in the world: 35 000 riders tackle the 105 km (65 mile) long course around the Cape Peninsula.

The Perseverance Tavern (near Parliament) is the oldest pub in Cape Town: it served its first drink way back in 1836.